What Is the Future of Hydrogen Power?

Carla Mooney

ReferencePoint
Press®

San Diego, CA

About the Author

Carla Mooney is the author of many books for young adults and children. She lives in Pittsburgh, Pennsylvania, with her husband and three children.

For more information, contact:
ReferencePoint Press, Inc.
PO Box 27779
San Diego, CA 92198
www.ReferencePointPress.com

Picture Credits:
Cover: Thinkstock.com
Maury Aaseng: 8, 11, 17, 22, 31, 36, 43, 49, 57, 61

LIBRARY OF CONGRESS CATALOGING-IN-PUBLICATION DATA

Mooney, Carla, 1970-
  What is the future of hydrogen power? / Carla Mooney.
    pages cm. -- (The future of renewable energy series)
  Audience: Grade 9 to 12.
  Includes bibliographical references and index.
    ISBN 978-1-60152-274-0 (hardback : alk. paper) -- ISBN 1-60152-274-6 (hardback : alk. paper)
  1. Hydrogen as fuel--Juvenile literature. 2. Power resources--Juvenile
literature. I. Title.
  TP359.H8M66 2013
  665.8'1--dc23
                                                                    2012020154

Contents

Foreword

What are the long-term prospects for renewable energy?

In his 2011 State of the Union address, President Barack Obama set an ambitious goal for the United States: to generate 80 percent of its electricity from clean energy sources, including renewables such as wind, solar, biomass, and hydropower, by 2035. The president reaffirmed this goal in the March 2011 White House report *Blueprint for a Secure Energy Future*. The report emphasizes the president's view that continued advances in renewable energy are an essential piece of America's energy future. "Beyond our efforts to reduce our dependence on oil," the report states, "we must focus on expanding cleaner sources of electricity, including renewables like wind and solar, as well as clean coal, natural gas, and nuclear power—keeping America on the cutting edge of clean energy technology so that we can build a 21st century clean energy economy and win the future."

Obama's vision of America's energy future is not shared by all. Benjamin Zycher, a visiting scholar at the American Enterprise Institute, a conservative think tank, contends that policies aimed at shifting from conventional to renewable energy sources demonstrate a "disconnect between the rhetoric and the reality." In *Renewable Electricity Generation: Economic Analysis and Outlook* Zycher writes that renewables have inherent limitations that can be overcome only at a very high cost. He states: "Renewable electricity has only a small share of the market, and ongoing developments in the market for competitive fuels . . . make it likely that renewable electricity will continue to face severe constraints in terms of competitiveness for many years to come."

Is Obama's goal of 80 percent clean electricity by 2035 realistic? Expert opinions can be found on both sides of this question and on all of the other issues relating to the debate about what lies ahead for renewable energy. Driven by this reality, *The Future of Renewable Energy* series critically examines the long-term prospects for renewable energy by delving into the topics and opinions that dominate and inform renewable energy policy and debate. The series covers renewables such as solar, wind, biofuels, hydrogen, and hydropower and explores the issues of cost and affordability, impact on the environment, viability as a replacement for fossil fuels, and what role—if any—government should play in renewable energy development. Pointed questions (such as "Can Solar Power Ever Replace Fossil Fuels?" or "Should Government Play a Role in Developing Biofuels?") frame the discussion and support inquiry-based learning. The pro/con format of the series encourages critical analysis of the topics and opinions that shape the debate. Discussion in each book is supported by current and relevant facts and illustrations, quotes from experts, and real-world examples and anecdotes. Additionally, all titles include a list of useful facts, organizations to contact for further information, and other helpful sources for further reading and research.

Visions of the Future: Hydrogen Power

When Jack Cusick drives, people point at his car. Cusick drives a 2008 Honda FCX Clarity, the world's first hydrogen-powered fuel cell electric vehicle (FCEV) intended for mass production. "We turn a lot of heads on the road and freeway. I get thumbs-ups from people, and occasionally I'll see someone bust out a camera phone and point it at me,"[1] said Cusick.

Cusick's car may look like an ordinary sedan, but this car may move the world closer to a future without petroleum. Instead of gasoline, a fuel cell powers the car by combining hydrogen and oxygen to make electricity. According to Honda, the FCX Clarity can be filled easily at a hydrogen pump and will drive 280 miles (451km) on a single tank of hydrogen. It gets higher fuel efficiency than a gasoline or hybrid car, approximately the equivalent of 74 miles per gallon (31.5km/L) of gasoline. Moreover, the car's only emissions are water and heat. In a world of dwindling fossil fuels, rising oil prices, and global warming concerns, a hydrogen-powered car has many people excited. "This is a must-have technology for the future of the earth," said Takeo Fukui, Honda's president. "Honda will work hard to mainstream fuel-cell cars."[2]

For Cusick, the FCX has become a part of daily life. He drives the car about 200 miles (322km) per week, mostly going to and from work and running errands. Fueling the car is easy, he says, although he is limited in where he can drive because hydrogen filling stations are scarce. Still, Cusick is thrilled to be driving the hydrogen-powered car. He explained:

When the opportunity to drive a Honda FCX Clarity FCEV presented itself, I jumped at the chance. The main benefit, obviously, is a smaller carbon footprint. More than that, though, is the opportunity to show the world that fuel-cell vehicles can work. I'm driving, parking, fueling, and traveling right alongside everyone else. I wanted to be a part of the future; I discovered that I'm actually a part of the present.[3]

What Is Hydrogen Power?

Hydrogen is the simplest and most common element in the universe. On earth, hydrogen is a colorless, odorless gas (H_2). Rarely found alone, it is usually bonded with other elements such as oxygen in water (H_2O) or carbon in methane (CH_4). To use it, hydrogen must be split from these other elements.

By itself hydrogen is not an energy source like natural gas or oil. Instead, hydrogen is a carrier, like electricity, that stores and delivers energy in a usable form. To use hydrogen as an energy carrier, scientists separate it from the other elements with which it is found. Separating hydrogen requires another energy source, which can be renewable like solar power or nonrenewable like natural gas.

Producing Hydrogen

Hydrogen can be separated from other elements using several technologies. Currently, the most common method is natural gas steam reforming, which accounts for about 95 percent of hydrogen produced in the United States today. Using this method, high-temperature steam separates hydrogen from methane in natural gas. This method is not ideal, because it uses nonrenewable natural gas as an energy source, and the process releases greenhouse gases into the atmosphere. Electrolysis, which uses an electric current to split water molecules into hydrogen and oxygen, is a cleaner method of separating hydrogen. Electrolysis requires electrical energy, which can be produced by fossil fuels or renewable sources such as wind,

Inside a Hydrogen Fuel Cell Car

The potential benefits of hydrogen fuel cell vehicles, which run on hydrogen gas rather than gasoline, include reducing dependence on foreign oil and lowering harmful emissions that contribute to climate change. But these benefits cannot be realized until fuel cell vehicles can realistically compete with conventional vehicles, and that cannot happen until several challenges are overcome. On the outside, hydrogen fuel cell cars look like any other cars. Where they differ is on the inside. The biggest difference is the fuel cell stack. It converts oxygen from the air and hydrogen gas stored onboard into electricity, which powers the electric motor that propels the car.

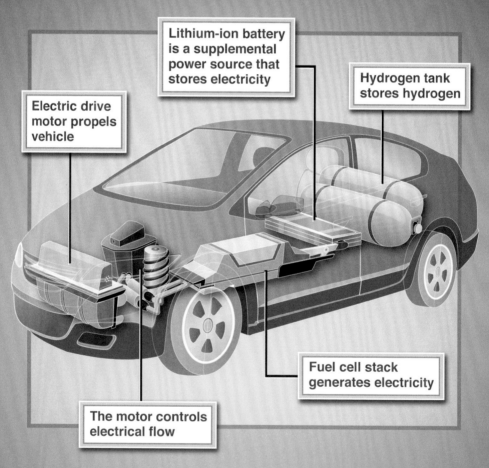

Lithium-ion battery is a supplemental power source that stores electricity

Hydrogen tank stores hydrogen

Electric drive motor propels vehicle

Fuel cell stack generates electricity

The motor controls electrical flow

Source: US Department of Energy, "Fuel Cell Vehicles," 2012. www.fueleconomy.gov.

solar, geothermal, or hydroelectric power. Hydrogen can also be produced by gasification, which converts coal or biomass into a gas that then reacts with steam to separate hydrogen. Several other technologies are also in various stages of development for hydrogen production.

Hydrogen power can also be produced in fuel cells, like the one that powers Honda's FCX Clarity. Fuel cells combine hydrogen with oxygen from the air to generate electricity, leaving heat and water as the only by-products. Hydrogen flows from a storage tank into the fuel cell, where a chemical reaction generates electricity and powers an electric motor. As long as hydrogen is supplied, the fuel cell will produce electricity and never lose its charge.

Uses for Hydrogen Power

Hydrogen is mainly used for industrial purposes today, but it has much potential as a fuel and power source in the future. Currently, the United States produces more than 9 million tons (8.2 million metric tons) of hydrogen annually. Most of it is used for industrial purposes, including in gasoline refining, cleaning semiconductors, and as an ingredient in fertilizer manufacturing. In the future, hydrogen has the potential to be used even more widely. One of the most promising uses of hydrogen is as a fuel for cars, buses, and other vehicles. Hydrogen can be used as a vehicle fuel in two ways. It can be burned similarly to how gasoline is burned in modified internal combustion engines, or it can be generated in a fuel cell that powers the vehicle. Several automakers have already developed hydrogen cars and plan to mass-produce them by 2015.

Scientists are also developing ways to use hydrogen-powered fuel cells in stationary applications. Hydrogen fuel cells the size of air-conditioning units can provide homes and buildings with reliable power around the clock. In Japan hydrogen fuel cells already power thousands of homes, and a few such fuel cells are at work in the United States. Larger fuel cells might also power large office buildings. The National Aeronautics and Space Administration put stationary hydrogen power to work on its space shuttles, using the abundant element and fuel cells for power, heat, and water. Fuel cells powered computers, life-support systems, and lighting on the shuttles. They also generated heat and produced water for the astronauts to drink.

Even small electronic devices might one day run on hydrogen fuel cells. Electronics giant Apple is working on laptops and smart phones powered by hydrogen fuel cells. These cells would last for weeks without needing to be refueled or recharged, like batteries need to be.

Advantages of Hydrogen

One of the biggest advantages of using hydrogen for fuel and power is its widespread availability. Taking advantage of local resources, regions rich in coal could generate hydrogen through coal gasification, while sunny regions could generate hydrogen through a solar electrolysis process.

Another significant advantage of hydrogen is that it is clean burning and virtually pollution free. When used in a fuel cell or in a modified internal combustion engine, hydrogen's only emissions are heat and water vapor. Using hydrogen instead of fossil fuels has the potential to reduce greenhouse gas emissions and other environmental pollutants. When using renewable resources to produce hydrogen, the entire process from production to end use has very low environmental impact.

Moreover, hydrogen power is versatile. Unlike other forms of renewable energy, it does not depend on weather conditions or time of day. What is more, once hydrogen is generated, it can be stored at power plants for future use when consumers need electricity.

Hurdles for Hydrogen

Although hydrogen offers many advantages, there are several hurdles that must be overcome before hydrogen becomes a mainstream energy source. One of the biggest hurdles facing hydrogen is cost. Separating hydrogen to make it useable is an expensive process. Currently, the cheapest way to separate hydrogen is natural gas steam reforming. However, this method releases carbon dioxide into the atmosphere. Electrolysis solves that problem but requires a substantial amount of energy to separate water's hydrogen and oxygen, and the platinum needed in the process is very expensive.

How Hydrogen Fuel Cells Work

Cars powered by hydrogen use polymer electrolyte membrane, or PEM, fuel cells. These fuel cells use oxygen from the air and hydrogen fuel that is stored onboard to produce electricity. The electricity drives a motor that propels the car. The diagram shows how a PEM fuel cell works.

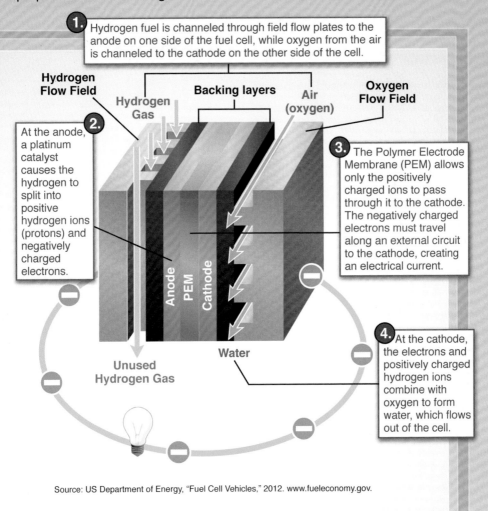

1. Hydrogen fuel is channeled through field flow plates to the anode on one side of the fuel cell, while oxygen from the air is channeled to the cathode on the other side of the cell.

Hydrogen Flow Field

Hydrogen Gas

Backing layers

Air (oxygen)

Oxygen Flow Field

2. At the anode, a platinum catalyst causes the hydrogen to split into positive hydrogen ions (protons) and negatively charged electrons.

3. The Polymer Electrode Membrane (PEM) allows only the positively charged ions to pass through it to the cathode. The negatively charged electrons must travel along an external circuit to the cathode, creating an electrical current.

Anode
PEM
Cathode

4. At the cathode, the electrons and positively charged hydrogen ions combine with oxygen to form water, which flows out of the cell.

Unused Hydrogen Gas

Water

Source: US Department of Energy, "Fuel Cell Vehicles," 2012. www.fueleconomy.gov.

Additionally, a significant investment in hydrogen distribution networks is required before widespread use can occur. Currently, there are few pipelines to transport hydrogen from processing plants to users. Instead, hydrogen distribution relies on more expensive and less efficient truck and tanker transportation. Additional investments would be needed for new hydrogen fueling stations to be built and for consumers to purchase new hydrogen-powered cars.

Hydrogen must also overcome storage hurdles to become more widely used in the transportation market. Hydrogen is the smallest and lightest atom in the universe. As a gas, hydrogen easily diffuses into materials and leaks from containers. Hydrogen molecules spread out easily, making the gas bulky to store. To contain hydrogen gas, it must be highly pressurized and stored in specialized leak-proof tanks. These challenges have caused hydrogen tanks in cars to be expensive, heavy, and unable to hold large loads of fuel. Smaller loads limit the driving range of hydrogen cars to fewer than 300 miles (483km) per tank. While automakers have recently demonstrated progress with some prototype vehicles traveling more than 300 miles on a single fill, this driving range must be achievable across different vehicle models and without compromising space, performance, and cost, or consumers will not buy hydrogen cars.

An Important Future

Despite the challenges, research that will solidify hydrogen power as an integral part of the world's renewable transportation fuel and energy future is ongoing. As the global demand for energy increases, fossil fuel alternatives must be developed. For hydrogen, the future may rest on the industry's ability to develop technology to produce fuel and energy economically from the world's most abundant element. According to David Hart, a consultant and director of the London-based sustainable energy consultancy E4tech and principal research fellow at Imperial College London, the world needs to develop energy carriers that are environmentally friendly, locally sourced, and able to store intermittent renewable energy. "There is only one common thread running through these, and that is hydrogen," said Hart. "While other energy carriers can assist in achieving some of these objectives, none of them meet all of the requirements. That is why even the major oil companies see hydrogen as a major part of the energy future."[4]

Chapter One

Is Hydrogen Power Affordable?

Hydrogen Power Is Affordable

Hydrogen power is an emerging energy alternative that will be more affordable in the future as technology improves and as production increases. The cost benefits of hydrogen power, however, have broader financial implications. Because hydrogen can be produced domestically, rather than being purchased abroad, the US economy will benefit through reduced dependence on foreign oil. And because hydrogen power emits fewer pollutants and greenhouse gases than fossil fuels do, costs to human health will be significantly lower—another factor that enhances the affordability of hydrogen power.

The Debate

Hydrogen Power Is Too Costly

Hydrogen power is costly and inefficient. Proven methods of separating hydrogen into a usable form are too expensive, and less costly methods are unproven. Even if hydrogen could be produced economically, the United States currently lacks the infrastructure to widely distribute it to consumers. Widespread use of hydrogen fuel would require significant up-front expenditures for new production plants, pipelines, and fueling stations. Even then, the high cost of hydrogen fuel cell vehicles would put them out of the reach of most consumers.

Hydrogen Power Is Affordable

"The price [of hydrogen] will come down as more fuel providers get into the field, as production methods such as electrolysis and other forms evolve, and as storage and compression technology is made more efficient."

—Peter Hoffmann, author and founder of the *Hydrogen & Fuel Cell Letter*.

Quoted in Jim Motavalli, "Questions for Peter Hoffmann: A Hydrogen Advocate Whose Time May Have Come," *New York Times*, February 2, 2012. www.nytimes.com.

The hydrogen power industry is young, but as it develops, hydrogen power promises to be an affordable energy alternative. Since 2000, technology for producing hydrogen and hydrogen fuel cell vehicles has become less expensive. The cost of fuel cell vehicles, in particular, has declined dramatically and is expected to decrease even more in the future. According to the Toyota Motor Corporation, the cost of making hydrogen fuel cell vehicles has dropped about 90 percent since 2005. "We're finding ways to reduce the cost through manufacturing improvements, and we expect to make a lot of gains,"[5] said Justin Ward, program manager for Toyota Motor Engineering & Manufacturing North America. As researchers develop and refine hydrogen production and fuel cell technologies, hydrogen's cost will fall even further in the future.

Innovation

In 2008 the manufacturing cost of a hydrogen fuel cell car was approximately $1 million. Automakers like Toyota predict that they can reduce the car's manufacturing cost to about fifty thousand dollars by 2015. Researchers are focusing on the hydrogen car's fuel tanks and fuel stacks, two of the car's most expensive components, to drive down the price of hydrogen cars.

Innovation to reduce fuel tank costs will decrease the cost of hydrogen vehicles. Many fuel tanks are wrapped in an expensive carbon-fiber textile to make the tank more sturdy, durable, and leakproof. Only a small number of suppliers worldwide manufacture the specialty tanks, driving up the cost. To reduce costs, automakers like Toyota are learning how to make the tanks in-house rather than outsourcing them. "We looked at what [outside suppliers] were doing and decided there was no way it would ever be possible to manufacture a fuel-cell vehicle under those circumstances," said Ward. "So we decided to bring the tank process in-house and do it ourselves."[6]

> **"We're finding ways to reduce the cost through manufacturing improvements, and we expect to make a lot of gains."[5]**
>
> —Justin Ward, program manager for Toyota Motor Engineering & Manufacturing North America.

More innovation in the design of the fuel cell stack, which provides the car's power, will further lower the cost of hydrogen fuel cell vehicles. The hydrogen car's fuel cell produces electrical energy through a chemical reaction that splits hydrogen and oxygen. To date, fuel cells have used the expensive metal platinum as a catalyst, a material that speeds up the chemical reaction. In order to lower fuel cell cost, researchers have found ways to reduce platinum use to about one-third of previous levels. Moreover, Toyota and the General Motors Company reported in 2010 that they have a goal of further reducing platinum from current levels of 1.06 ounces (30g) per fuel cell vehicle to about 0.35 ounces (10g) by 2015.

Discovery of New Catalysts

While innovation is reducing platinum in hydrogen fuel cells, entirely replacing the expensive catalyst has the potential to reduce the cost of hydrogen fuel cells and cars dramatically. "With hydrogen being touted as a clean burning fuel that generates no CO_2, creating cheaper and better catalysts has become a big and important field now. The main push is toward more earth-abundant materials than the rare metals like platinum,"[7] said Christopher Chang, associate professor of chemistry at the University of California–Berkeley.

In 2011 scientists at the Los Alamos National Laboratory demonstrated a new catalyst in hydrogen fuel cells. The catalyst used carbon, iron, and cobalt instead of platinum. It performed well in tests, generating electrical currents comparable to platinum fuel cells and showing favorable durability. "For all intents and purposes, this is a zero-cost catalyst in comparison to platinum, so it directly addresses one of the main barriers to hydrogen fuel cells,"[8] said Piotr Zelenay, a Los Alamos researcher.

Volume Production

True cost savings will be realized once the volume of hydrogen fuel cell vehicle manufacturing increases. To date, auto manufacturers have only made the cars in small quantities. Mass production will lead to further cost reductions and allow auto manufacturers to take advantage of volume discounts from auto part suppliers and cost savings from manufacturing larger quantities. "We plan to come to market in 2015, or earlier, with a vehicle that will be reliable and durable, with exceptional fuel economy and zero emissions, at an affordable price,"[9] said Irv Miller, a Toyota Motor North America spokesperson.

The 2015 hydrogen cars are expected to cost approximately fifty thousand dollars, which is the equivalent of a luxury sedan. Auto manufacturers predict volume production will push down the price of hydrogen cars even further, eventually making them competitive with conventional cars.

Infrastructure Solutions

One of hydrogen's biggest cost challenges is the lack of infrastructure and fueling stations to distribute the fuel. After production, hydrogen must be transported from processing plants to fueling stations and users. Pipelines are the least expensive way to deliver hydrogen, but there are very few dedicated hydrogen pipelines in the United States—less than 1,200 miles (1,931km). Instead, most hydrogen is distributed by more expensive and less efficient trucks and tankers. To minimize costs until more affordable pipelines and transportation solutions are developed, hydrogen can be produced in decentralized locations. Limiting how far hydrogen is transported to reach consumers will decrease its distribution costs.

Falling Costs for Hydrogen Fuel Cell System

With advances in fuel cell technology the cost of hydrogen fuel cells has steadily decreased and that downward trend is expected to continue. Innovation in fuel stack design, the fuel cell's most expensive part, has been a significant driver in lowering fuel cell cost. By 2010, fuel cell stacks dropped to $25/kWh, approximately 49 percent of total fuel cell cost.

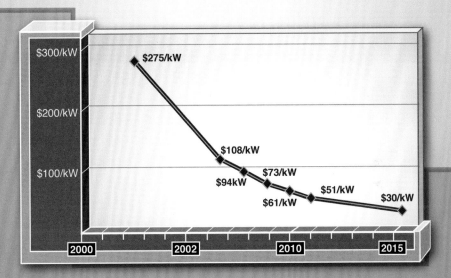

Source: Jacob Spendelow and Jason Marcinkoski, "Fuel Cell System Cost—2010." Department of Energy, September 16, 2010. www.hydrogen.energy.gov.

In addition, small rollouts of fueling stations in targeted areas would reduce infrastructure expenses until the hydrogen power industry further matures. The cluster approach, meaning building small groups of fueling stations in the same geographic area, is already being used successfully in Southern California, where Honda leases two hundred FCX Clarity cars to consumers. General Motors believes that the cluster approach will allow a hydrogen distribution network to be built at a fraction of the cost of a nationwide rollout. The company says that if twelve thousand hydrogen stations were built in the largest one hundred American cities, there would be a hydrogen station within 2 miles (3.2km) of 70 percent of Americans. "We don't think about this as a nationwide deployment on Day 1, where everything has to be covered immediately,"[10] said Britta Gross, General Motor's manager for hydrogen and electrical infrastructure. Gross cited

Los Angeles as an example, saying that a network of forty hydrogen stations would cover the initial needs of the city and would cost only $80 million. Steven Chalk, deputy assistant secretary for renewable energy at the US Department of Energy (DOE), said in 2008, "Five years ago we would have said that we need to launch hydrogen nationally but we now think that this cluster idea is the way to go. The way to do that is to concentrate in areas where you have critical mass."[11]

Improving Hydrogen Storage

As hydrogen storage technology improves, hydrogen's costs will decrease. Currently, the cost of pressurizing hydrogen or cooling it to very cold temperatures for storage is expensive. Leakproof tanks that are sturdy and secure enough to contain highly pressurized or liquid hydrogen are also heavy, expensive, and limited in size.

Because storage costs are a concern, researchers are developing new ways of storing hydrogen. In December 2011 the DOE granted over $7 million to four research teams working on hydrogen storage technology. "Targeted investments in cutting-edge hydrogen storage technologies will spur American ingenuity, accelerate breakthroughs, and increase our competitiveness in the global clean energy economy,"[12] said secretary of energy Steven Chu about the research grants. If these technologies are successful, they will reduce the price of hydrogen fuel tanks in vehicles and at fueling stations.

> "We plan to come to market in 2015, or earlier, with a vehicle that will be reliable and durable, with exceptional fuel economy and zero emissions, at an affordable price."[9]
>
> —Irv Miller, Toyota Motor North America spokesperson.

Hydrogen Reduces Hidden Costs

Dependence on fossil fuels carries many indirect costs that do not exist with hydrogen power. Burning fossil fuels releases pollutants that have been linked to acid rain, global warming, and human health impacts. Air pollutants can cause or aggravate a number of health conditions, including chronic respiratory disease, lung cancer, and heart disease, and can cause damage to the brain, liver, nerves, and kidneys. As a result, society incurs significant health-care costs. According to a 2009 report by the National Academy of Sciences, burning fossil fuels—primarily oil and coal, which release significant amounts of air pollution—costs the United States about $120 billion annually in health-care costs.

Using hydrogen power generated from carbon-free sources like wind and solar power reduces pollution and emission of greenhouse gases. According to the Fuel Cell & Hydrogen Energy Association, a single hydrogen fuel cell vehicle can save more than 3 tons (2.7 metric tons) of carbon dioxide emissions annually, as compared with a conventional vehicle. Reducing these pollutants will bring down society's costs for pollution-related health care.

In addition, using hydrogen power can reduce the security costs the United States incurs to protect its foreign oil interests. These costs can be extremely volatile due to political instability around the world. Prior to the Iraq War in 2001, the National Defense Council Foundation estimated that the fixed costs of defending Middle Eastern oil were approximately $50 billion annually. In a follow-up study, the foundation estimated that oil defense costs soared to $137.8 billion in 2006. In contrast, hydrogen power can be produced locally, eliminating these massive expenditures.

An Affordable Choice

When evaluating hydrogen power's affordability, it is important to consider the broad range of costs incurred by fossil fuels versus the broad range of cost benefits for hydrogen power. Technological advances are steadily lowering the cost of hydrogen power, and this will continue well into the future. In addition, hydrogen power reduces society's indirect health-care and security costs, making it an attractive and affordable energy choice. "In the long term, hydrogen and fuel-cell vehicles look like a major part of the [energy] solution,"[13] said Larry Burns, General Motor's vice president for research, development, and strategic planning.

Hydrogen Power Is Too Costly

"Concerns about the viability of hydrogen stem from the need to build an entirely new production, distribution, and refueling infrastructure to support a hydrogen-fueled fleet . . . and the current high cost of fuel cells and fuel cell vehicles."

—David L. Greene and Howard H. Baker Jr., Center for Public Policy, and Steven E. Plotkin, Argonne National Laboratory.

David L. Greene et al., "Reducing Greenhouse Gas Emissions from U.S. Transportation," Pew Center on Global Climate Change, January 2011. http://cta.ornl.gov.

In 2007 the city of Charlottetown on Canada's Prince Edward Island announced that it would add two hydrogen-powered buses to its fleet. The buses would shuttle passengers around town, emitting no emissions or greenhouse gases. Once the buses were in use, town officials quickly discovered that they were expensive to operate. Planned wind turbines on the island could not produce enough hydrogen to power the buses, so the town was forced to truck in hydrogen fuel from Quebec, an expensive alternative. Despite initial funding from the Canadian government and the hydrogen fuel supplier, money to operate the buses ran out in 2011, forcing the town to put the buses in storage. In March 2011 Charlottetown announced that the hydrogen bus program was too expensive to maintain and it was shipping the buses back to the manufacturer.

While the idea of hydrogen power may be attractive, Charlottetown's experience demonstrates that making hydrogen power cost-competitive will not be easy. Although the cost of hydrogen vehicles has decreased in recent years, hydrogen fuel cell vehicles and their operation are still too expensive for most communities and consumers. In addition to the cost of the vehicles, the world lacks the infrastructure to produce and distribute hydrogen at an affordable price. Building the necessary plants, pipelines, and fueling stations would be an undertaking that is simply too expensive for many communities to afford. "There is a significant economic hurdle in hydrogen. We can't provide it on a retail fueling basis to be cost-competitive with gasoline, not today,"[14] said Puneet Verma, director of the Chevron Corporation's hydrogen research and development efforts.

Lack of Infrastructure

Perhaps the greatest barrier to widespread use of hydrogen power is the size and cost of the infrastructure needed to transport and distribute hydrogen from production plants to filling stations and consumers around the country. Today more than 170,000 fuel stations distribute gasoline across the United States. Millions of miles of pipelines and thousands of tanker trucks carry gasoline from refineries to local filing stations around the country, a distribution system that took a century to develop.

Pipelines are the least expensive way to deliver hydrogen from production plants to filling stations, but there are very few dedicated hydrogen pipelines in the United States, less than 1,200 miles (1,931km). Hydrogen cannot be distributed through existing oil or natural gas pipelines because hydrogen gas makes the steel tubing brittle and weakens the welded connections. Getting hydrogen gas from production plants to users would require construction and installation of expensive, specially treated pipes. According to estimates by the National Research Council, the total cost of deploying a national network of hydrogen pipelines could run as high as $200 billion.

> "There is a significant economic hurdle in hydrogen. We can't provide it on a retail fueling basis to be cost-competitive with gasoline, not today."[14]
>
> —Puneet Verma, director of Chevron's hydrogen research and development efforts.

Without a dedicated pipeline network, most hydrogen today is delivered as either a cryogenic liquid in hydrogen tankers or barges or as a compressed gas carried by truck, train, ship, or barge in high-pressure tube trailers. Transporting hydrogen gas via truck or tanker is very expensive because of the amount of pressure required to store the hydrogen and is primarily used for distances of 200 miles (322km) or less. Liquefied-hydrogen tankers

Hydrogen Fueling Stations Are Too Scarce

Hydrogen is not an affordable alternative fuel because it is too difficult and expensive for consumers to find and use. As of 2012, there were fewer than sixty hydrogen fueling stations across the United States, concentrated in only a few states, leaving many Americans without access to affordable hydrogen fuel.

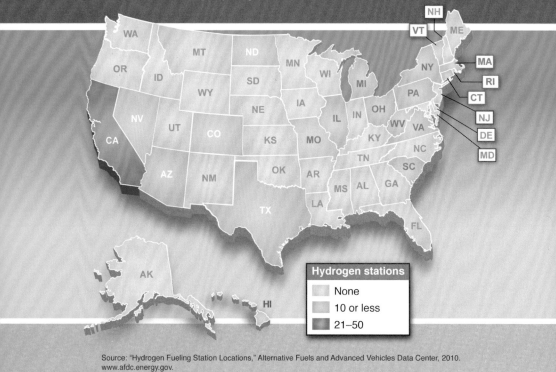

Hydrogen stations
- None
- 10 or less
- 21–50

Source: "Hydrogen Fueling Station Locations," Alternative Fuels and Advanced Vehicles Data Center, 2010. www.afdc.energy.gov.

allow hydrogen to be transported over longer distances, but the liquefaction process is also expensive.

Once transported from production plants, hydrogen must also be safely stored and dispensed at refueling stations. Because hydrogen molecules are so light and spread out in their natural state, hydrogen gas must be highly pressurized when stored to reduce the storage space needed and to minimize leaks. Existing gasoline storage tanks cannot be used to safely store hydrogen. Instead, expensive leakproof tanks must be constructed at fueling stations to hold it. Because of the high cost of building these hydrogen storage tanks and special fueling centers, very few hydrogen filling stations exist. There are fewer than 60 hydrogen stations in the United States and only 180 stations worldwide, which severely limits hydrogen's availability to consumers. The high cost of building more stations will likely limit the number of hydrogen stations built in the near future. This in turn may limit consumer use of hydrogen vehicles. "Car drivers can only benefit from the advantages of technology if there are enough hydrogen filling stations available,"[15] said Dieter Zetsche, Daimler's chair and the director of its Mercedes-Benz Cars unit.

The Production Process

Although hydrogen exists throughout the world, it cannot be used as an energy carrier unless it is separated first from feedstock sources (raw materials) such as water, methane, or natural gas. Currently, there are several methods for producing or extracting hydrogen, all of which are expensive. Most hydrogen, approximately 95 percent, is produced by steam reforming of natural gas, whereby high temperatures and pressure break the natural gas hydrocarbons into their hydrogen and carbon elements. According to the DOE, the cost of producing hydrogen from natural gas for a fuel cell vehicle can run as high as forty dollars per million BTUs, making hydrogen about four times as expensive as gasoline at the pump.

Another way of producing hydrogen, electrolysis, is even more costly. Electrolysis produces hydrogen by electrically splitting water into its basic elements, hydrogen and oxygen. Because electrolysis requires an electrical current to run through the water, the cost of electrolysis depends on the cost of electricity. Using electricity generated from fossil fuel sources is less expensive, but to make hydrogen power truly renewable, electrolysis needs to be powered by renewable sources of energy such as wind turbines or solar panels. The higher cost of electricity generated by these renewable sources drives the cost of hydrogen higher, making it difficult to compete on price with less expensive fossil fuel–generated electricity.

Hydrogen Cars

The current cost of hydrogen vehicles is more than double the cost of many conventional cars. Even if auto manufacturers can deliver on their promised projections of a fifty-thousand-dollar hydrogen car by 2015, this vehicle cost will still be too expensive for the majority of consumers. And there is no guarantee that automakers will be able to deliver on reducing the cost of hydrogen cars, because the two main cost drivers, the vehicle's fuel cell and hydrogen storage tank, are still expensive.

> "Hydrogen has probably fallen back. That's because hydrogen is the most challenging in terms of fuel production, vehicle technology and infrastructure deployment."[18]
>
> —Roland Hwang, an automobile expert with the Natural Resources Defense Council, an environmental group.

To date, automakers have used platinum as the catalyst material in the fuel cells that power hydrogen cars. Platinum is a rare metal that is more expensive than gold. Although scientists are working to reduce the amount of platinum used in hydrogen fuel cells, current versions still require at least 1.06 ounces (30g) of platinum per fuel cell, with some companies reporting that they use roughly 2.1 to 2.8 ounces (60g to 80g) of platinum per fuel cell vehicle. At the current platinum price of about sixty dollars per gram, platinum costs alone can range from eighteen hundred dollars up to forty-eight hundred dollars per fuel cell.

Although scientists hope to reduce platinum use further, there is no guarantee that the technology needed to do so will be successful. In addition, platinum is a rare material. If production of hydrogen fuel cells using platinum were to increase significantly, the resulting increase in demand for platinum would deplete supplies and send the price of the precious metal soaring, further increasing the cost of hydrogen fuel cells. Burt Richter, a physicist and the former director of the Stanford Linear Accelerator Center at Stanford University, points out a further problem with platinum: "It isn't just the fact that it's expensive, it's that it's not there. Right now, it takes 60 grams of platinum per fuel cell. The entire world supply of platinum wouldn't be enough for the cars produced in the U.S. alone."[16]

Onboard storage of hydrogen fuel is another contributor to the high cost of hydrogen vehicles. Designing a fuel tank that can hold hydrogen gas in amounts that allow a driving range of more than 300 miles

(483km) has always been a challenge. Hydrogen atoms are the smallest and lightest in the universe. Because storing bulky hydrogen gas in its natural state would require a tank too large to be practical, most hydrogen vehicles use onboard storage tanks that hold hydrogen gas compressed at hundreds of times atmospheric pressure. Most companies have chosen to use modern carbon-fiber tanks, which can safely hold the highly pressurized hydrogen. But the cost of these carbon-fiber tanks is still hundreds of times more than a conventional gas tank. According to the DOE website, "The cost of on-board hydrogen storage systems is too high, particularly in comparison with conventional storage systems for petroleum fuels. Low-cost materials and components for hydrogen storage systems are needed, as well as low-cost, high-volume manufacturing methods."[17] Until hydrogen car manufacturers find a more affordable way to build hydrogen cars and storage tanks, the cost of hydrogen vehicles will remain too high for the average consumer.

Competition with Other Technologies

Other technologies may be more affordable for consumers, edging out hydrogen's place in the transportation market. Auto manufacturers are continually improving the efficiency of existing gasoline- and diesel-powered engines. Advances in hybrid cars and plug-in, battery-powered vehicles are gaining momentum and making these choices more affordable and attractive to consumers. Research breakthroughs and government subsidies of biofuels have also presented a challenge to hydrogen fuel. Roland Hwang, an automobile expert with the Natural Resources Defense Council, believes that electric cars and biofuels have taken the edge away from hydrogen. "Hydrogen has probably fallen back. That's because hydrogen is the most challenging in terms of fuel production, vehicle technology and infrastructure deployment,"[18] said Hwang.

Chapter Two

How Does Hydrogen Power Impact the Environment?

Hydrogen Power Is Environmentally Friendly

Hydrogen power has two primary advantages over fossil fuels in terms of environmental impact. The processes to obtain hydrogen release few greenhouse gases—especially when produced using other renewable energy sources. And when used to power vehicles, hydrogen is virtually emission and pollutant free, releasing only water vapor and heat. Hydrogen also saves natural resources by being more energy efficient than gasoline, which allows hydrogen-powered cars to use less fuel to travel the same distance.

The Debate

Hydrogen Power Harms the Environment

Hydrogen is only as clean as the energy producing it, and most hydrogen power is currently produced from nonrenewable fossil fuels such as natural gas. Although hydrogen emits only water vapor when used for energy, the burning of fossil fuels to produce hydrogen releases greenhouse gases and toxic air pollutants into the atmosphere. Also troubling, hydrogen production consumes significant amounts of scarce water resources and may damage the atmosphere with unavoidable hydrogen leaks.

Hydrogen Power Is Environmentally Friendly

"Fuel cell and hydrogen technologies . . . are a crucial part of the portfolio of advanced energy technologies that will help achieve the nation's oil and greenhouse gas reduction goals."

—Nine US senators.

Letter to US Senate, March 21, 2012. www.fchea.org.

At the Coca-Cola Company's San Leandro, California, bottling plant, the company unveiled a fleet of thirty-seven hydrogen fuel cell forklifts and nineteen hydrogen pallet jacks in 2012. The company purchased the hydrogen vehicles in order to use more fuel-efficient equipment and reduce its fleet's emissions. Rene Hom, Coca-Cola Northwest Region vice president of field operations and supply chain, said:

> We are dedicated to expanding our AFV [alternative fuel vehicle] fleet and continue to look for innovative ways to move and deliver Coca-Cola products throughout California. The addition of hydrogen-powered forklifts and pallet jacks to our current 125-AFV fleet in California further strengthens our on-going commitment to energy conservation, recycling and zero waste, while driving down operating costs and improving process efficiencies.[19]

The San Leandro plant's switch to a hydrogen-powered fleet is one step toward reducing the world's greenhouse gas emissions and, as a result, reducing global warming. Hydrogen power is a clean, efficient, environmentally friendly energy alternative. Hydrogen production releases fewer greenhouse gases than fossil fuel production, especially when renewable energy sources are used. In addition, when hydrogen is used to power vehicles, virtually no greenhouse gas or pollutants are emitted. According to Peter Hoffmann, editor and publisher of the *Hydrogen Fuel Cell Letter*, hydrogen energy is "on its way to becoming a major environmentally benign, sustainable, renewable component of the world's energy mix for both transportation and stationary applications."[20]

Reducing Greenhouse Gases

Hydrogen can help reduce carbon dioxide in the atmosphere, especially when used to power road vehicles. Burning fossil fuels to power vehicles releases carbon dioxide gas into the atmosphere, which is one of the most common greenhouse gases and is widely believed to contribute to global warming. According to a 2011 report by the International Energy Agency, the transportation sector contributed 23 percent of worldwide carbon dioxide emissions from fossil fuel combustion in 2009. Of those emissions, road vehicles such as cars and trucks accounted for the vast majority of carbon dioxide emissions. The problem is expected to worsen in the future; the International Energy Agency predicts that global demand for road transport will rise 40 percent by 2035.

> "We have a vehicle technology today where you can make the fuel onsite using renewables, where the process is zero emissions."[21]
>
> —Orth Hedrick, director of product planning for Kia Motors America.

In comparison, hydrogen fuel cell vehicles significantly reduce greenhouse gas emissions because hydrogen emits only heat and water from the vehicle's exhaust system. As the number of hydrogen fuel cell vehicles on the road increases, the overall reduction of greenhouse gases will also increase. The National Academy of Sciences predicts that 2 million hydrogen vehicles could be on the road in 2020, growing to 25 million vehicles by 2030. These projections translate into greenhouse gas emission reductions for light-duty vehicles, which have a gross vehicle weight of less than 8,500 pounds (3,855kg), of 20 percent by 2035 and more than 60 percent in 2050.

Although fuel cell vehicles have no emissions when in use, hydrogen vehicles are not completely carbon-free, because the process of producing the hydrogen that powers them emits some greenhouse gases. Most hydrogen today is produced using fossil fuels such as natural gas and coal, with methods that release some greenhouse gases. Yet even when the emissions from fuel production are counted, hydrogen fuel still releases fewer harmful greenhouse gases than petroleum refining for use in vehicles. The DOE calculated that fuel cell vehicles using hydrogen produced from natural gas reduce total greenhouse gas emissions by 60 percent as compared with gasoline-powered internal combustion engine vehicles.

In the future, when hydrogen fuel is made from less carbon-intensive production methods, there will be significantly higher reductions of greenhouse gases. When hydrogen is produced via electrolysis powered by renewable sources, it creates little to no greenhouse gases, making it one of the most environmentally clean sources of fuel. When produced with renewable energy, hydrogen's total greenhouse gas emissions from production to use in a fuel cell vehicle are lower than total emissions from traditional gasoline, biofuels, or hybrid-powered vehicles. "We have a vehicle technology today where you can make the fuel onsite using renewables, where the process is zero emissions,"[21] said Orth Hedrick, director of product planning for Kia Motors America.

Carbon Capture and Storage Technology

Although producing hydrogen from emission-free, renewable sources is the long-term goal, most hydrogen is currently produced from fossil fuels, which emit greenhouse gases. Two common methods, natural gas steam reforming and coal gasification, both release carbon dioxide during the production process. Even hydrogen produced via electrolysis releases emissions when the electricity used in the production process is generated by fossil fuels.

To reduce carbon dioxide emissions, scientists are working on producing hydrogen with methods that use carbon capture and storage (CCS) technologies, which capture, transport, and store carbon dioxide emissions before they are released into the air. With CCS, the carbon dioxide produced by hydrogen production is transported to a storage site and then typically injected under high pressure into deep underground caverns, where it cannot escape into the atmosphere and contribute to global warming. CCS technologies can reduce carbon dioxide emissions from hydrogen production to near zero.

CCS technology combined with coal gasification has great potential to produce hydrogen affordably with significantly reduced carbon dioxide emissions. In the United States coal is an attractive feedstock for hydrogen because it is relatively inexpensive and found in large quantities. To produce hydrogen, gasification turns coal into a gas that consists of hydrogen along with other elements. A series of steps separates the hydrogen from the other elements. With CCS the carbon dioxide emitted during production would be stored underground and not released into the atmosphere, reducing carbon dioxide emissions by as much as 90 percent as compared with a coal-fueled power plant.

Better Air Quality

In addition to reducing greenhouse gases, using hydrogen to fuel vehicles or generate electricity reduces the amount of harmful air pollutants released when fossil fuels are burned. Burning gasoline in conventional vehicle engines or at electrical power plants releases toxic pollutants, including particulate matter, nitrogen oxides, and sulfur dioxide. These pollutants have been linked to the creation of smog, acid rain, and negative human health impacts.

Unlike gasoline or diesel, burning hydrogen in vehicles releases little to no toxic emissions or particulates into the air. Instead, vehicles running on hydrogen fuel release only water and heat. "Hydrogen has always been the Holy Grail because they are zero-emissions vehicles. That has always been the primary goal,"[22] said Gloria Bergquist, a spokesperson for the Alliance of Automobile Manufacturers.

When used to generate electricity in power plants, hydrogen can also improve air quality. According to a 2012 report by the American Lung Association, coal-fired power plants release more toxic air pollutants, including arsenic and lead, than any other US industrial pollution source. "Power plant pollution kills people. It threatens the brains and nervous system of children. It can cause cancer, heart attacks and strokes,"[23] said Charles D. Connor, president and CEO of the American Lung Association. In contrast, burning hydrogen to generate electricity is virtually emission free and releases no pollutants.

Hydrogen Power Reduces Carbon Dioxide Emissions

Using hydrogen reduces the amount of carbon dioxide emissions in the atmosphere, believed to be a leading cause of global warming. Comparing the carbon content of different fuels, hydrogen carries no carbon. As a result, it releases no carbon dioxide.

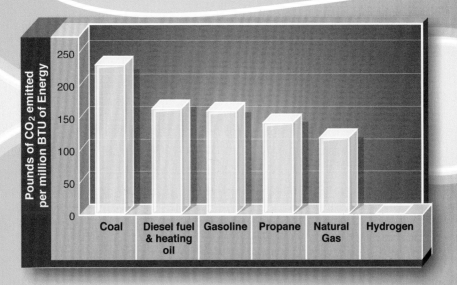

Source: "Frequently Asked Questions: How Much Carbon Dioxide (CO_2) Is Produced When Different Fuels Are Burned?," US Energy Information Administration, April 28, 2011. http://205.254.135.7/tools/faqs/faq.cfm?id=73&t=11.

Energy Efficiency

Hydrogen fuel cell vehicles are more energy efficient than gasoline vehicles, achieving the equivalent of 60 to 70 miles per gallon (25.5 to 29.8 km/L), compared with gasoline-powered cars that average 20 to 30 miles per gallon (8.5 to 12.8 km/L). This efficiency allows consumers to use less fuel to drive the same distances, which conserves natural resources and reduces harmful environmental effects from fuel production.

Hydrogen fuel cells are more efficient because they convert stored energy directly into heat and electricity, using a one-step chemical reaction. With only one step, less energy is lost during the conversion process. In comparison, internal combustion engines generate energy through a multiple-step process, With each step, more energy is lost, reducing the overall energy efficiency of the engine. According to the DOE, a hydrogen vehicle fuel cell averages about 60 percent energy efficiency, while the internal combustion engines in gasoline-fueled cars have a much lower 25 percent efficiency rate.

A test of hydrogen-powered municipal buses in Basel, Switzerland, demonstrated hydrogen's energy efficiency. Operators using the hydrogen buses reported that the vehicles used half the fuel of conventional buses. Basel also implemented a test of hydrogen-powered street cleaners in 2009 and concluded that the efficient vehicles were a good fit for hydrogen fuel cell power. "This type of vehicle is usually driven at very low load, about five to six kilometers an hour. And fuel cell systems have high efficiency at low speeds,"[24] says Christian Bach, head of the internal combustion engines lab at the Swiss Federal Laboratories for Materials Science and Technology. Engineers reported that by switching to hydrogen, they were able to reduce the vehicles' energy consumption by 50 percent.

> "Hydrogen has always been the Holy Grail because they are zero-emissions vehicles. That has always been the primary goal."[22]
>
> —Gloria Bergquist, spokesperson for the Alliance of Automobile Manufacturers.

A Responsible Choice

Whether used in vehicles or to produce electricity, hydrogen power is an environmentally friendly energy carrier. Amid rising concerns about air pollution, greenhouse gases, and global warming, hydrogen power emits no harmful gases or pollutants. Even when fossil fuels are used to produce hydrogen, the net amount of greenhouse gases and pollutants released is still lower than those released by fossil fuel power plants. In addition, hydrogen's superior efficiency as compared with gasoline allows less of it to be used, conserving energy and the earth's natural resources.

Hydrogen Power Harms the Environment

"Hydrogen right now is not as clean as it sounds."

—Giorgio Rizzimi, director of the Center for Automotive Research at Ohio State University.

Quoted in Thomas K. Grose, "Hype or Hope?," *ASEE Prism*, September 2010, p. 47.

The environmental benefits of hydrogen power have been vastly overstated. Hydrogen is only as clean as the energy producing it, and the majority of hydrogen power is currently produced from nonrenewable fossil fuels such as natural gas and coal. Hydrogen can either be extracted from fossil fuels or made using electrolytic processes powered by fossil fuels. Either way, the burning of these fossil fuels to produce hydrogen releases greenhouse gases and toxic air pollutants into the atmosphere.

Production Methods Release Greenhouse Gases

Although hydrogen is an abundant element, it is rarely found alone and is usually bonded with other elements. Therefore, hydrogen used for energy must be separated from these elements using one of several technologies. The most common method of producing hydrogen, natural gas steam reforming, releases carbon dioxide and other pollutants into the air, which reduces hydrogen's environmental benefits. According to a Reason Foundation 2007 report, if the United States replaced 20 percent of its vehicles with hydrogen cars, carbon dioxide emissions would only slightly decrease, from 1.67 billion tons (1.51 billion metric tons) annually to 1.63 billion tons (1.48 billion metric tons). This is because the emissions released when hydrogen fuel is produced and transported by truck to fueling stations offset a large portion of the emissions saved by using hydrogen vehicles. "Hydrogen isn't the quick-fix we've been led to believe it could be," said

Adrian Moore, vice president of research at the Reason Foundation and the study's project director. "Producing and transporting hydrogen for use in fuel-cell cars requires significant amounts of conventional energy and therefore won't reduce greenhouse gas emissions. When you look at the facts you see hydrogen isn't a solution to global warming."[25]

Carbon-Friendly Technology Expensive and Unproven

Scientists have tried to develop more environmentally friendly methods of producing hydrogen. So far, none of these has gone beyond computer models and research labs. For example, hydrogen produced via electrolysis that uses renewable sources of electricity like wind or solar power has zero or near-zero greenhouse gas emissions and is very attractive in theory. Yet less than 5 percent of hydrogen today is actually produced using this method. This does not seem likely to change in the near future, since there are currently no commercial scale demonstrations of zero-emission hydrogen-production plants running.

The cost of producing hydrogen with renewable energy is simply too expensive and will probably remain so in the future. According to the Fuel Cell & Hydrogen Energy Association, electricity produced from solar-powered hydrogen electrolysis costs approximately ten times more than fossil fuel–generated electricity. "A sustainable energy choice that no one can afford is not sustainable at all,"[26] said Jens Nørskov of the DOE's SLAC National Accelerator Laboratory and Stanford University.

Hydrogen Production Is Inefficient

Extracting hydrogen from feedstock sources is an inefficient process that can sometimes require more energy than it produces. Although hydrogen can be found worldwide, it is always bonded to another element and must be separated before it can be used as an energy carrier. The extraction process requires an enormous amount of energy from fossil fuels or renewable energy sources.

The most common method of producing hydrogen, natural gas steam reforming, actually uses more energy than it produces. According to Jon Maddy of the Hydrogen Research Unit at the University of Glamorgan in

Wales, using steam reforming to extract hydrogen from natural gas loses 20 percent of the energy used during processing, leaving users with less electricity from hydrogen than could have been produced directly from the natural gas. "You might as well use natural gas in the first place,"[27] said Maddy. According to Maddy, it is actually more energy efficient to use hydrocarbons like natural gas as fuel or to generate electricity than going through the trouble of separating hydrogen from the natural gas.

Hydrogen Leaks May Harm Atmosphere

In addition to the harmful greenhouse gases and pollutants released by fossil fuels during hydrogen production, hydrogen itself may pose a danger to the atmosphere. It is impossible to manufacture, store, and transport hydrogen without some escaping into the atmosphere. As more hydrogen is used, escaped hydrogen could accumulate in the atmosphere, depleting the ozone layer and contributing to global warming.

In one study, researchers from the California Institute of Technology found that a substantial increase in hydrogen production could potentially damage the upper atmosphere. They estimated that if hydrogen replaced fossil fuels as the world's main energy source, 132 billion to 265 billion pounds (60 billion to 120 billion kg) of hydrogen could be released into the atmosphere. Those numbers represent a doubling or tripling of the amount currently released through human and natural sources. Although leaked hydrogen's effect is still uncertain, scientists believe it could accumulate in the air and damage the ozone layer, a layer of the atmosphere that shields earth from the sun's harmful ultraviolet radiation. In this way hydrogen would be like chlorofluorocarbons used in air-conditioning and refrigeration in the mid- to late-1900s, which leaked into the atmosphere and depleted the ozone layer.

> "Producing and transporting hydrogen for use in fuel-cell cars requires significant amounts of conventional energy and therefore won't reduce greenhouse gas emissions. When you look at the facts you see hydrogen isn't a solution to global warming."[25]
>
> —Adrian Moore, vice president of research at the Reason Foundation.

Hydrogen Production Diverts Scarce Water Resources

Hydrogen production, particularly the method known as electrolysis, uses a significant amount of water—already a scarce resource worldwide. During production, water from lakes or reservoirs is pumped to the hydrogen plant, where it is separated into hydrogen and oxygen elements. This water is consumed, meaning it is used up and not returned to its source. A significant quantity of water is also withdrawn from lakes or reservoirs for use in cooling production equipment, especially during thermoelectrically powered electrolysis. Once cooling is complete, this water is returned to its source. But while it is in use, less water is available for local communities and farms that rely on the same lakes and reservoirs for drinking water and irrigation. As the demand for hydrogen power increases, more water will be needed and competition for an already limited water supply will increase.

Fuel	Production Method	Water Consumption	Water Withdrawals
Gasoline	Refining	2.5 gal/gal	2.5 gal/gal
Hydrogen	Steam methane reforming	4.6 gal/kg–1	4.6 gal/kg–1
Hydrogen	Electrolysis (thermoelectric)	27 gal/kg–1	1100 gal/kg–1
Hydrogen	Electrolysis (hydroelectric)	950 gal/kg–1	0 gal/kg–1

Note: Units listed are gallons of water per gallon of gasoline (gal/gal) or gallons of water per kilogram of hydrogen (gal/kg–1).

Source: Michael E. Webber, "The Water Intensity of the Transitional Hydrogen Economy," Center for International Energy and Environmental Policy, Jackson School of Geosciences, University of Texas at Austin, September 20, 2007. http://iopscience.iop.org.

A 2011 study by European researchers came to a similar conclusion. The study reported that if hydrogen were produced on a large-scale basis, leaks would deplete the ozone layer. High levels of hydrogen could potentially cause atmospheric chemical changes that would extend the lifetime of methane, one of the most potent greenhouse gases. Methane traps twenty-five times more heat in the atmosphere than carbon dioxide over its lifetime of approximately eight to nine years. Increasing methane's lifetime will result in more greenhouse gas damage to the atmosphere and ozone layer.

Safety Issues

In addition to its negative effects on the environment, hydrogen may also pose a safety threat to humans. Hydrogen is a light, extremely flammable gas. It is odorless, colorless, and tasteless, making it unable to be detected by human senses. If hydrogen leaks without being detected, it could cause a potentially devastating fire. In 1937 the German passenger zeppelin *Hindenburg* burst into flames over Lakehurst, New Jersey, killing thirty-six people. The zeppelin was filled with highly flammable hydrogen gas. Officials blamed the fire on a spark that caused leaking hydrogen gas to ignite. Since the infamous disaster, the safety of using highly flammable hydrogen as a fuel, particularly in vehicles, has been questioned. "The concern will always be there, let's face it, because hydrogen is very flammable,"[28] said Peter Hoffmann.

For other flammable fuels like natural gas, producers add odorants to the gas to help humans smell it in the event of a leak. This cannot be done with hydrogen in fuel cell vehicles, because current odorants contaminate fuel cells. Hydrogen is also more combustible than gasoline, making it a dangerous fire hazard during leaks or vehicle crashes. Patrick Coyle, a process chemist, explained, "[Hydrogen] burns at a much wider range of concentrations in the atmosphere than propane, and requires less energy to ignite. This means that hydrogen is much more likely to catch fire than are hydrocarbon fuels currently in use."[29] Because of these concerns, many do not believe that hydrogen-powered vehicles and fuel cells are safe for humans or the environment.

Water Use

In many parts of the world, water is a precious and limited resource. In the southwestern United States, for instance, farmers and city dwellers compete for water, and their needs are pitted against the needs of wildlife. This competition would be magnified by any future increases in hydrogen production.

Producing hydrogen consumes a significant amount of water. Hydrogen production by electrolysis uses water directly as a feedstock, separating the water molecules into hydrogen and oxygen. Hydrogen production also uses water indirectly as a cooling fluid or to generate steam in fossil fuel–powered electricity plants. As the demand for hydrogen increases, the water needed to produce hydrogen will also increase.

According to one study by researchers at the University of Texas–Austin, hydrogen production using thermoelectric-powered electrolysis was significantly more water intensive than gasoline production. The study found that for every kilogram of hydrogen produced, thermoelectrically powered electrolysis consumes 27 gallons (102L) of water as a feedstock and for cooling. In comparison, gasoline refining consumes 2.5 gallons (9.5L) of water for every gallon of gasoline produced.

> **"Hydrogen is much more likely to catch fire than are hydrocarbon fuels currently in use."[29]**
>
> —Patrick Coyle, a process chemist.

As hydrogen production increases, the strain on water resources will increase. Researchers at Sandia National Laboratories, a government research facility, have noted that hydrogen production from natural gas reforming is very water intensive and requires more water than petroleum refining. Because water is an integral part of hydrogen production and electricity generation, increased reliance on hydrogen energy in the future will have serious consequences on water resources and availability. "The U.S. energy infrastructure depends heavily on the availability of water, and there is cause for concern about the availability of that water as we look toward future demands on limited water resources,"[30] the scientists concluded.

Environmental Challenges

Hydrogen is not the environment-saving fuel and energy carrier that many have promised. While hydrogen itself releases few emissions, the production and transport of hydrogen can be a dirty process, contributing greenhouse gases and pollutants to the atmosphere. In addition, the benefits of using hydrogen must be evaluated against the potential environmental dangers of hydrogen leaks and the draining of scarce water resources around the world.

Chapter Three

Can Hydrogen Power Ever Replace Fossil Fuels?

Hydrogen Power Can Reduce Fossil Fuel Use

Hydrogen power is a renewable, domestically produced energy alternative that can reduce worldwide use of fossil fuels. Hydrogen power can be used in place of fossil fuels in many energy applications, including transportation, electricity production, and heating. Hydrogen power can be generated and stored for future use, making it a reliable source of energy. As technology improves, hydrogen power will become more cost effective and widespread, allowing it to replace even more fossil fuels in the coming years.

The Debate

Hydrogen Power Is Not a Viable Replacement for Fossil Fuels

Hydrogen power is not a viable replacement for fossil fuels. The repeated failures of hydrogen conversion technologies to meet cost, reliability, and durability targets make it unlikely hydrogen will be able to replace fossil fuels meaningfully now or in the future. In addition, limited market demand and distribution infrastructure for hydrogen will hinder production and make it difficult for consumers to find and use significant amounts of hydrogen.

Hydrogen Power Can Reduce Fossil Fuel Use

"Hydrogen and fuel cell technologies are an essential part of America's energy solution. Commercial fuel cells will deliver clean, efficient energy at home and at work, create hundreds of thousands of American jobs and, together with other technologies, eliminate the need for gasoline for passenger vehicles."

—Joint Statement of the Electric Drive Transportation Association, the National Hydrogen Association, and US Fuel Cell Council.

The Electric Drive Transportation Association et al., "Hydrogen and Fuel Cell Industries Join Call to Increase Clean Energy Investment," Fuel Cell Markets, June 11, 2010. www.fuelcellmarkets.com.

Hydrogen power has the potential to reduce fossil fuel use around the world. Fossil fuels, which include natural gas, oil, and coal, provide the majority of the world's energy for cars, electricity, and heating. Historically, fossil fuels have been an easy-to-use and reliable energy source. A major problem with fossil fuels, however, is that they are not renewable resources. Once used, fossil fuels cannot be replaced. Some experts believe that the world has already reached peak production for fossil fuels or will reach it shortly. As fossil fuel reserves become depleted, they will become more limited and expensive. As a result, it will cost more to drive cars, heat homes, and purchase products manufactured with fossil fuels.

Rising world energy demand will hasten that process. According to estimates from the DOE, the worldwide demand for energy will rise by more than 50 percent in the next twenty years. In addition, the number of cars that use primarily petroleum-based liquid fuels worldwide is predicted to double by 2050.

The concerns with fossil fuels have led to an increased focus on sources of alternative energy, such as hydrogen power. "There has to be a shift from fossil fuels to hydrogen,"[31] said Vijay Bhatkar, an Indian scientist involved in clean energy research.

A Key Source of Renewable Energy

Unlike fossil fuels, hydrogen power is a renewable resource. Enormous quantities of hydrogen exist on earth, although they are locked up in water, hydrocarbons, and other organic matter. When hydrogen is separated from these compounds using methods like electrolysis that are powered by wind, biomass, and solar power, hydrogen is considered infinitely renewable. As long as the sun shines, the wind blows, and rain falls, hydrogen will be available on earth.

Always available, hydrogen can be used in place of fossil fuels in transportation, electricity production, and heating. Unlike solar or wind power, which are dependent on weather conditions or time of day, hydrogen power is available twenty-four hours a day, every day. Hydrogen production plants can produce fuel that can be stored for future use.

Hydrogen is also versatile. Unlike hydrogen, other renewable energy sources like solar panels and wind turbines only generate electricity, which cannot easily be used by the transportation sector. In comparison, hydrogen can be burned in internal combustion engines just like gasoline or generated by fuels cells that can be used in cars, trucks, planes, trains, boats, and other vehicles. "Our path to the fuel of the future will take us from clean conventional fuels and first- and second-generation biofuels to hydrogen and electricity produced from renewable sources,"[32] said the German automaker Daimler in a statement.

Reducing Oil Consumption

Hydrogen is a promising alternative to oil, especially in the transportation market. Around the world, oil is one of the most widely used fossil fuels. According to BP's 2010 *Statistical Review of World Energy*, consumption of oil accounted for 34 percent of the world's primary energy usage in 2010, increasing 3.1 percent over the prior year. The vast majority of oil is used for transportation. In the United States transportation accounted for more than 70 percent of the total US oil demand, consuming over 14 million barrels per day. With more cars and airplanes in use, demand is expected to rise even further.

Hydrogen can replace oil used for transportation fuel in two ways. Similar to how gasoline is burned to power vehicles, hydrogen can be burned as a fuel in modified internal combustion engines. It can also be used in fuel cells to power electric motors. Fuels cells are well suited for transportation, because they are highly efficient and have a short refueling time that is comparable to that of petroleum-based fuels.

Hydrogen fuel cell vehicles have the potential to provide the benefits of battery-run electric cars. They operate quietly, have rapid acceleration, and have low maintenance requirements. Along with these benefits, hydrogen fuel cell vehicles can drive for longer distances and recharge in a shorter period than electric battery-run cars.

The automotive industry has recognized the potential of hydrogen fuel cell vehicles and invested billions of dollars in research and development to produce affordable, efficient vehicles powered by hydrogen. After years of development, the industry claims that mass-produced hydrogen cars will be ready for sale by 2015. "Fuel-cell technology is viable and ready for the mass market," Toyota's Chris Hostetter, said at the 2011 opening of a hydrogen filling station in Torrance, California. "Building an extensive hydrogen refueling infrastructure is the critical next step in bringing these products to market."[33]

> "There has to be a shift from fossil fuels to hydrogen."[31]
>
> —Vijay Bhatkar, an Indian scientist involved in clean energy research.

Hydrogen-Powered Electricity

In addition to being used to power vehicles, hydrogen is a promising way to store and carry electricity generated from renewable energy sources. Currently, fossil fuels generate most US electricity, with coal being the most common source. In 2010, 45 percent of the nation's almost 4 trillion kilowatt-hours of electricity used coal as its energy source. Natural gas and oil generated 24 percent and 1 percent of electricity, respectively.

Big Corporations Switching to Hydrogen Power

Many top US and Canadian companies are switching to hydrogen fuel cell stationary power and forklifts and other vehicles—collectively saving millions of dollars in electricity costs and dramatically reducing carbon emissions. This shift suggests strong potential for reducing fossil fuel use—or even eliminating it—in the future.

	Fuel Cell Stationary Power	Fuel Cell Forklifts	Fuel Cell Vehicles
Production Facilities			
Coca-Cola	X	X	X
Gills Onions	X		
Nestlé Waters		X	
Pepperidge Farm	X		
Sierra Nevada Brewery	X		
Super Story Industries		X	
Bridgestone-Firestone		X	
Nissan North America		X	
Kimberly-Clark		X	
Michelin	X		X
Distribution Facilities			
Martin-Brower		X	
Sysco		X	
United Natural Foods Inc.		X	
U.S. Foodservice		X	
FedEx	X	X	X
UPS	X		X
Retail & Grocery Stores			
Cabela's	X		
IKEA			X
Staples	X		
Walmart	X	X	
Central Grocers		X	
H-E-B		X	
Price Chopper	X		
Star Market	X		
Wegmans		X	
Whole Foods Market	X	X	
Telecom			
Sprint	X		
Verizon	X		
Motorola	X		
Hospitality			
Hilton Hotels	X		X
Starwood Hotels and Resorts	X		
Corporate Headquarters/Data Centers			
eBay	X		
First National Bank of Omaha	X		
Fujitsu	X		
Cox Enterprises	X		
Chevron	X		
Cypress Semiconductor	X		

Source: "The Business Case for Fuel Cells 2011: Energizing America's Top Companies," Fuel Cells 2000, November 2011. p. 68. www.fuelcells.org.

Hydrogen can be used in tandem with renewable energy sources such as wind turbines or solar panels to provide electricity and reduce the need for fossil fuels. One of the challenges facing renewable energy sources like wind and solar power is their intermittent nature, which limits their availability and reliability as a source of electricity. Used together with hydrogen, electricity generated by these intermittent energy sources can be stored and then used when needed, providing a reliable electricity supply. Wind turbines or solar panels provide electricity to an electrolyzer, a device that converts water into hydrogen gas. Then the gas can be stored until it is used. When electrical power is needed, the hydrogen gas is pumped into a fuel cell that produces electricity and water.

As the use of renewable energy increases, the need for hydrogen will also increase. Gladwyn De Vidts, chief strategic officer of AEG Power Solutions, explained: "The significant increase of these renewable energies thus creates the need for energy storage or transformation, and hydrogen and/or methane production are now developing faster and faster as clean energy storage solutions."[34]

Waste hydrogen gas from chemical plants even has the capability to produce electricity. Since 2009 the European utility Enel has operated a power plant near Venice, Italy that runs on 100 percent hydrogen. The company said that it uses hydrogen supplied from a nearby petrochemical facility in Porto Marghera. Enel built a 1.24-mile (2km) pipeline to transport the hydrogen, a by-product of the manufacturing process that would otherwise go to waste, from the petrochemical facility to their power plant. In July 2009 the Enel hydrogen power plant generated enough electricity for twenty thousand households. "The initial input of electricity onto the grid from the fully operational plant is a world-beating technological achievement,"[35] Enel said in a statement.

Stationary Fuel Cells Provide Heat and Power

In addition to providing electricity from power plants to the electrical grid, stationary hydrogen fuel cells can provide heat and electricity to individual homes and businesses. Currently, fossil fuels generate heat and electricity for most US homes. Stationary hydrogen fuel cells can replace fossil fuels when installed as the primary or backup power for homes or businesses. Fuel cells provide clean, efficient, and reliable power, and when the electric grid fails, they can provide power off-grid.

In Japan more than two thousand homes use hydrogen-powered fuel cells for hot water and electricity. A fuel cell the size of a suitcase sits outside the home, next to a water heater tank. The fuel cell uses oxygen from the air and hydrogen from natural gas piped to the home for heat and cooking to generate electricity. At the same time the fuel cell gives off enough warmth to heat household water. "Fuel cells are wonderful devices because they provide combustionless, pollution-free electricity,"[36] said Masanori Naruse, a Japanese homeowner using a fuel cell power system. The Japanese government has set a goal for 25 percent of Japanese homes to use hydrogen-powered fuel cells by 2020.

> "Fuel-cell technology is viable and ready for the mass market."[33]
>
> —Chris Hostetter, Toyota's US group vice president for advanced planning.

Hydrogen's ability to power an entire building was on display at Expo 2012, a world fair held in Yeosu, South Korea. The expo featured the Korea Pavilion, the world's first hydrogen-powered building. Two stationary hydrogen fuel cells that powered the building had the capacity to generate 50 kilowatts of electricity. Experts estimate that if the Korea Pavilion were operated continuously for a year, its hydrogen fuel cells would save approximately 400 tons (363 metric tons) of carbon-dioxide emissions annually.

A Promising Future

As concern over the price, availability, and environmental effects of fossil fuels rises, the benefits of hydrogen as a replacement for fossil fuels becomes more and more apparent. Although hydrogen's potential may be greatest in powering vehicles, its versatility will allow this abundant element to be used increasingly for electricity generation, stationary power, and other applications in the future. "From transportation to construction, national defense to industrial design and more, fuel cell and hydrogen technologies are entering a new era of opportunity and growth,"[37] said Morry Markowitz, of the Fuel Cell & Hydrogen Energy Association.

Hydrogen Power Is Not a Viable Replacement for Fossil Fuels

"Thirty years from now, the American economy will still be dependent on the most affordable, efficient fuel sources available—oil, coal, and natural gas."

—Thomas J. Pyle, president of the Institute for Energy Research.

Thomas J. Pyle, "Just Look at the Numbers," March 8, 2011, comment on Amy Harder, "30 Years from Now: How Will We Power America?," *Energy Experts Blog, National Journal,* March 7, 2011. http://energy .nationaljournal.com.

For two years the CityCat H2 street sweeper has been busy scrubbing the streets of Basel, Switzerland, as part of a pilot project to test the feasibility of hydrogen-powered vehicles in everyday life. Despite eighteen months of development before launching, the hydrogen sweeper encountered numerous problems and breakdowns. The fuel cell system broke down and had to be replaced. Other components, including the voltage converter, the electric motor drive, and two cooling water pumps, also malfunctioned and needed to be replaced. Finally, a team of researchers from Empa, the Swiss federal laboratory for materials science and technology, who studied the hydrogen vehicles concluded that the vehicles were simply not ready for wide release. "It became clear relatively quickly that the fuel-cell system, which had been developed as a one-off specially for the project, was not yet ready for use in a real-life setting," said project leader Christian Bach, the head of Empa's internal combustion engines laboratory. "On top of that, the various safety systems kept interfering with each other and bringing everything to a halt."[38]

As demonstrated in Basel, hydrogen power is not yet ready for real-world use, and researchers trying to develop new hydrogen technology are still a long way from reaching that goal. For the foreseeable future, then, hydrogen cannot be considered a viable replacement for fossil fuels.

Production Scale Too Limited

Although hydrogen production shows potential, it is not developing fast enough to be an effective replacement for fossil fuels in the near future. Hydrogen power remains a tiny fraction of overall energy produced and consumed. According to the National Renewable Energy Laboratory, the United States used 98 quadrillion Btus (British thermal units) of energy in 2010. Of that, 83 percent came from fossil fuels: oil, coal, and natural gas. According to the US Energy Information Administration (EIA), hydrogen contributes only approximately 1 quadrillion Btus of energy annually, or about 1 percent of the United States' energy needs. In fact, most of the hydrogen produced in the United States is not used for energy. Instead, 90 percent is used for petroleum refining or in the petrochemical industry. According to the EIA, "When hydrogen is used as a fuel or energy carrier rather than as an industrial chemical, substantially more hydrogen production capacity would have to be developed."[39]

The world demand for energy is expected to increase, with consumption projected to rise by 36 percent by 2035. Several factors are driving the increase. The world population is projected to grow 25 percent in the next twenty years. In addition, people use more energy as standards of living improve in many countries. In developed countries people are consuming more energy as they drive cars further, live in bigger homes, and use an expanding array of electronic devices.

Hydrogen cannot meet current energy needs; it is likely it will fall even further behind in the future as energy demand increases. According to analysts from energy company Chevron, "Fossil fuels will continue to provide the majority of the world's energy supplies for decades to come. Even under the most aggressive climate policy scenario presented by the International Energy Agency, fossil fuels are still expected to contribute at least 50 percent of the world's energy supplies in 2035."[40]

Infrastructure Not in Place

One of the biggest roadblocks for widespread adoption of hydrogen power is the lack of infrastructure to transport and distribute it to users around the country. There is currently no national system to transport

47

hydrogen from production plants to filling stations. "Infrastructure is a huge hurdle to acceptance,"[41] said Chao-Yang Wang, head of the Electrochemical Engine Center at Pennsylvania State University, who has redirected his center's research efforts from hydrogen to electric batteries.

In order for hydrogen fuel cell vehicles to become widely adopted, consumers will also need access to convenient, local fueling stations. In the United States there are few hydrogen refueling stations. According to the DOE's Alternative Fuels and Advanced Vehicles Data Center, there were fifty-six hydrogen-fueling stations across the United States as of March 2012, and these were concentrated in only four states. Major oil companies have been reluctant to set up hydrogen fueling tanks at existing gas stations because of the cost and a lack of demand. According to Joseph Romm, a senior fellow at the Center for American Progress and a former DOE official, the lack of convenient fueling stations is a significant barrier to the adoption of hydrogen. He believes that few consumers will buy hydrogen cars without a convenient place to refuel their cars. In return, without knowing there is a reliable market for the vehicles that will use hydrogen fuel, there is little incentive for car companies to build the fueling stations.

> **"When hydrogen is used as a fuel or energy carrier rather than as an industrial chemical, substantially more hydrogen production capacity would have to be developed."[39]**
>
> —US Energy Information Administration.

The difficulty of using hydrogen vehicles without an adequate hydrogen-fueling infrastructure was highlighted when the Hyundai Motor Company took its Tucson Fuel Cell Electric Vehicle on a demonstration trip across the United States, traveling more than 4,500 miles (7,242km) from San Francisco to New York in 2011. The Tucson could travel more than 400 miles (644km) on a tank of pressurized hydrogen, but finding a station to refuel the hydrogen car proved to be a challenge. At several points during the trip, hydrogen refueling was unavailable, so the car's demonstrators had containers of hydrogen shipped to them for refueling. "The stations weren't available, so when we could we had industrial hydro-

Hydrogen Fuel Cell Demand Far Behind Other Renewables

Other clean energy technologies may have a more promising future at replacing fossil fuels than does hydrogen. Billions of dollars have been invested in hydrogen research programs, yet the industry has made little progress in developing commercially viable technology and remains a much smaller sector than other technologies. Biofuels, wind power, and solar power are currently leading the way to replace fossil fuels worldwide and this trend is projected to continue in the future.

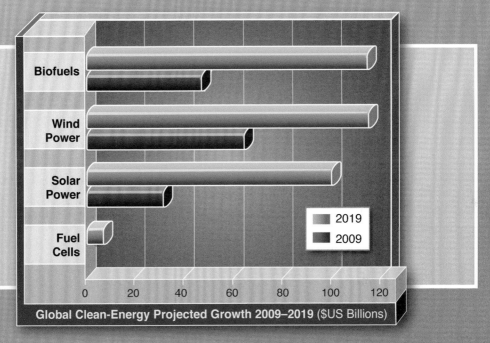

Global Clean-Energy Projected Growth 2009–2019 ($US Billions)

Source: "Assessment of the Economic Impact of the Canadian Hydrogen and Fuel Cell Sector," Ference Weicker and Company LTD, March 26, 2010. www.empr.gov.ca.

gen cylinders of the type used by welders and jewelry makers shipped to us at Hyundai dealers along the route. Then we used our own equipment to pressurize the hydrogen and get it into the form the car could use,"[42] said Zafar Brooks, a Hyundai spokesperson. Although automakers may have the capability to produce hydrogen cars in larger quantities by 2015, Hyundai officials say that the lack of hydrogen stations may slow or halt planned rollouts.

Competition from Alternatives

In the race to replace fossil fuels, hydrogen is moving too slowly and may lose out to competing alternative technologies. Billions of dollars have been invested in hydrogen research programs, yet the industry has made little progress in developing commercially viable technology. General Motors says that it has invested $2 billion in hydrogen technology, yet it only has a test fleet of one hundred fuel cell vehicles on the road to show for its investment.

Other alternative energy sources may overtake hydrogen as a replacement for fossil fuels. Biofuels are already replacing oil in the transportation sector, with the potential to replace even more oil in the future. Electric and plug-in hybrid cars have been faster to develop and provide a cheaper alternative to hydrogen fuel cell vehicles. While automakers predict a fifty-thousand-dollar retail price for hydrogen cars in 2015, Scott Grasman, an associate professor of systems engineering at the Missouri University of Science and Technology, believes the current cost of a hydrogen vehicle would be at least double that price. In comparison, the electric Nissan Leaf's base price in 2012 was about $35,000, dropping to close to $27,500 after accounting for a federal tax credit for purchasers. In 2010 Senate testimony, David Sandalow, an assistant secretary at the DOE, believes that the United States should move beyond hydrogen and concentrate on other alternative transportation technologies. "We need to focus in on those [technologies] that have extraordinarily high potential, and that, in my opinion, is electric drive,"[43] said Sandalow.

> "We're going to be moving away from hydrogen-fuel cells for vehicles. We asked ourselves, 'Is it likely in the next 10 or 15, 20 years that we will convert to a hydrogen car economy?' The answer, we felt, was 'no.'"[44]
>
> —Steven Chu, Secretary of Energy.

Secretary of energy Steven Chu and the White House agree that other alternative energy technologies may have a more promising future in replacing fossil fuels than does hydrogen. Chu and his department said that electric vehicles and plug-in hybrids were the surest way for the United States to reduce its dependence on foreign oil, while hydrogen technology would take too long to become a viable alternative. As a result, the White House has proposed to cut federal spending on hydrogen vehicle research. "We're going to be moving away from hydrogen-fuel cells for vehicles," said Chu. "We asked ourselves, 'Is it likely in the next 10 or 15, 20 years that we will convert to a hydrogen car economy?' The answer, we felt, was 'no.'"[44]

Durability and Reliability Problems

Hydrogen fuel cells will not be ready for widespread use until scientists are able to design fuel cell systems that perform as well as or better than traditional engines over the life of the vehicle. Currently, hydrogen fuel cells are good for approximately 75,000 miles (120,700km), which is only about half of the lifetime of internal combustion engines in conventional gasoline vehicles.

For fuel cell vehicles to compete with conventional cars, they also need to be able to operate in a variety of conditions. To date, hydrogen fuel cells have demonstrated problems operating in cold weather. This occurs because fuel cell systems contain water, which can freeze at low temperatures and must achieve a certain temperature for full performance. In order to compete effectively with gasoline vehicles, they would need to be able to operate fully in sub-freezing temperatures. "Fuel cell failure can occur through many different mechanisms. . . . New materials, new manufacturing processes and new designs are required to improve the durability of fuel cells,"[45] said Tom Fuller, a professor in the Georgia Institute of Technology's School of Chemical and Biomolecular Engineering, who is studying why fuel cells fail.

Hydrogen power is too costly and inefficient to compete effectively with fossil fuels. The technology to produce hydrogen at a reasonable price and the infrastructure to distribute it efficiently simply does not exist. There is no reason to believe this will change in the near future, meaning it cannot be seen as a realistic replacement for fossil fuels.

Chapter Four

Should Government Play a Role in Developing Hydrogen Power?

Government Should Have a Role in Hydrogen Power Development

For decades the government has made investments in energy, from subsidizing the exploration and extraction of fossil fuels to building nuclear power plants. These investments have helped fledgling industries develop and mature into sustainable, self-sufficient energy alternatives. In the same way, government support of clean energy alternatives such as hydrogen will help the world meet its energy challenges in a renewable, environmentally sound way.

The Debate

Government Should Not Be Involved in Developing Hydrogen Power

Government involvement in the hydrogen power industry is both unnecessary and harmful. History shows that government involvement in any energy technology frequently has negative effects. Hydrogen technology needs to develop in the free market, where market forces will decide whether it is a viable source of energy. Previous government attempts to subsidize the energy industry have failed, often resulting in negative and unintended consequences.

Government Should Have a Role in Hydrogen Power Development

"Government support has been and should continue to be an essential component in the growth of emerging energy sources, enabling U.S. technology innovation, job creation, and economic expansion."

—Nancy Pfund, managing partner of DBL Investors, a venture capital firm that invests in renewable energy ventures.

Quoted in DBL Investors, "Subsidies to New Energy Sources Are at Lowest Point in U.S. History," September 23, 2011. www.dblinvestors.com.

Hydrogen power is a promising energy source. It is renewable and environmentally friendly, and it reduces the country's dependence on imported oil. Hydrogen will also create jobs and bring economic benefits to local communities. Like many new technologies, the hydrogen power industry needs government support to help it grow into a sustainable, commercial industry. "Fuel cells and hydrogen technologies are transforming the energy network through distributed generation of clean, efficient and reliable power using a broad range of domestic fuels," said Ruth Cox, president and executive director of the Fuel Cell & Hydrogen Energy Association. "Today, the U.S. is the leader in fuel cell and hydrogen technologies, but we are at grave risk of losing our lead to competition in Europe and Asia."[46]

Staying Competitive with Other Countries

Around the world, the governments of many countries support the production and use of hydrogen power. Often, governments subsidize hydrogen production and research and development efforts through tax credits, loan guarantees, and grants. In Germany the government announced that it would provide 200 million euros between 2011 and 2014 to support research into energy storage, including that needed for hydrogen technology. "Germany may be in a unique position (to transform its energy system) because not only is there a consensus in society but also the technological competency,"[47] said Stephan Reimelt, head of GE Energy Germany at an energy conference in Berlin.

One of the companies benefiting from the investment is Enertrag, which operates one of Germany's first hybrid plants that generates wind power and converts it into hydrogen, which is stored and used for electricity. "My personal wish is that we help create the energy turning point and that wind power-to-hydrogen will take on a leading role," said Werner Diwald, an Enertrag board member. "The politicians are very interested in what we are doing here."[48]

The United States has historically been a leader in alternative energy and hydrogen power research. However, other countries have increased their support for developing hydrogen technology into a viable energy industry, and the United States must keep pace if it wants to avoid falling behind. In a joint statement, the Electric Drive Transportation Association, the National Hydrogen Association, and the US Fuel Cell Council called for the US government to increase its investment in clean hydrogen technology:

> "Federal and state governments have partnered with private industry and invested billions of dollars to position America as the leading supplier and consumer of fuel cell and hydrogen energy technologies. R&D funding, tax credits and other progressive policies have already created thousands of jobs."[51]
>
> —Fuel Cell & Hydrogen Energy Association.

The industry and government have had a strong partnership in developing hydrogen and fuel cell technologies, although federal investment has been decreasing in recent years. Going forward, a clarification of priorities is needed. To achieve our national goals for increased security and reduced pollutants, the U.S. must expand its commitment to the clean energy options that hydrogen and fuels provide. We have learned from other advanced energy opportunities lost that it will be more expensive to buy these technologies back from foreign competitors if we let them finish what the U.S. has started.[49]

A Level Playing Field

Government support and subsidies are a critical part of establishing an energy industry. The United States has a long history of supporting emerging industries. "Subsidies and government support have been part of many key industries in U.S. history—railroads, oil, gas and coal, aviation,"[50] said Damien LaVera, a DOE spokesperson. Fossil fuels have received hundreds of billions of dollars in government funding over many years. In the early twentieth century, government money helped support the hydroelectric power industry by contributing to the construction of dams. In addition, the government invested $100 billion in tax dollars for the development of nuclear power.

In the United States the government has supported hydrogen power by offering tax credits for installing hydrogen fueling equipment and purchasing hydrogen fuel cell vehicles. Federal and state governments have also supported hydrogen through investment in research and development and loan guarantees to companies developing hydrogen and fuel cell technologies. In 2003 President George W. Bush introduced the five-year, $1.2 billion Hydrogen Fuel Initiative. The initiative included $720 million in funding to develop technologies and infrastructure to produce, store, and distribute hydrogen for use in fuel cell vehicles and electricity generation. Congress has also passed the Energy Policy Act of 2005 and the 2007 Energy Independence and Security Act, which call for research and development of hydrogen and fuel cell technology and the related infrastructure. In addition to federal support of hydrogen, several states have passed energy acts that give tax exemptions and credits that promote infrastructure development for stationary hydrogen power technology.

These existing policies have been successful in making the United States one of the world leaders in hydrogen power development. According to the Fuel Cell & Hydrogen Energy Association, "Federal and state governments have partnered with private industry and invested billions of dollars to position America as the leading supplier and consumer of fuel cell and hydrogen energy technologies. R&D funding, tax credits and other progressive policies have already created thousands of jobs."[51]

Specifically, research and development funding have helped build the hydrogen market and encouraged private business owners and consumers to invest in hydrogen power technology and infrastructure. "These programs just level the playing field for what oil and gas and nuclear industries have enjoyed for the last 50 years," said Rhone Resch, president of the Solar Energy Industries Association. "Do you have to provide more policy support and funding initially? Absolutely. But the result is more energy security, clean energy and domestic jobs."[52]

Reduces Risks for Private Investors

Private investment in any new technology is risky, but energy and fuel production is especially challenging. It is capital intensive and requires large up-front investments in research and development, building production plants, and distribution networks. These costs act as a barrier for private investors in the hydrogen power industry. In Germany research from consulting firm A.T. Kearney shows that producing hydrogen currently costs two to four times more than Germany pays for imported gas. "Incentives will be necessary to help the technology reach market maturity,"[53] said Kurt Oswald, an A.T. Kearney partner. Diwald estimates that the hydrogen industry would need a government investment of between 700 million and 1 billion euros to help build the market in Germany. He says that seeing this large investment from the government, likely in the form of tariffs or state subsidies, would encourage private companies and investors to also invest in Germany's hydrogen industry.

Support from the government through research and development funding, loan guarantees, and tax credits can reduce risks for private investors and encourage them to invest in hydrogen power development. Several private automakers have invested heavily in the hydrogen industry, with a focus on developing hydrogen vehicles. These expensive investments are risky without a viable network to produce and distribute hydrogen fuel. The government can reduce the risk to these companies by investing in the needed production and distribution channels. Said

Government Subsidies Are Essential

The oil and gas and nuclear industries developed into mature, sustainable industries thanks in large part to generous subsidies over many decades. The same must be done for the hydrogen industry, although the same level of support has not yet materialized.

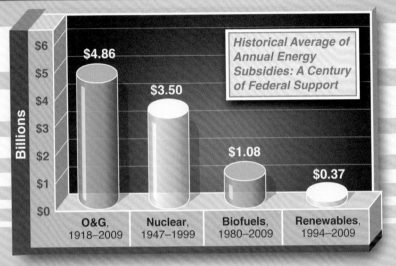

Historical Average of Annual Energy Subsidies: A Century of Federal Support

Source: Nancy Pfund and Ben Healy, "What Would Jefferson Do? The Historical Role of Federal Subsidies Shaping America's Energy Future," DBL Investors, September 2011, p.7. http://i.bnet.com.

Charles Freese, executive director of GM Fuel Cell Activities, "GM [General Motors] has invested more than $1.5 billion in fuel cell technology and we are committed to continuing to invest. . . . As we approach a costly part of the program, we will require government and industry partnerships to install a hydrogen infrastructure and help create a customer pull for the products."[54]

In Denmark the government has been an integral partner in developing the country's hydrogen industry. Since 2001 the Danish government has been a solid supporter of hydrogen fuel cell research and has provided millions of dollars in funding. In 2011 the government's funding of hydrogen research was estimated to be more than 30 million euros (or about $39 million).

In 2012 the Danish government announced a new energy plan, called Energy Plan 2020, which aims to help the country establish a foundation for hydrogen power. The plan's goal is for Denmark to establish a hydrogen fuel infrastructure that is functional and sustainable by 2020, allowing the country to achieve energy independence by 2050. The plan focuses heavily on hydrogen-powered transportation, bringing more hydrogen fuel stations to Denmark, and supporting companies that adopt hydrogen fuel. The plan will also give financial support to companies that build hydrogen fuel cells and vehicles to make hydrogen cars more affordable for consumers.

Denmark also plans to invest in other hydrogen energy projects, including residential and industrial fuel cells. "The new Danish hydrogen support initiatives follow years of continued and increasing public support for fuel cells and hydrogen (FCH) research, development and demonstration in Denmark,"[55] said Hydrogen Link, a national network for advancing the use of hydrogen for transport in Denmark.

> "Our industry needs continued government support to cross the chasm and achieve broad-scale commercial deployment. . . . We can't afford to risk throwing away the considerable efforts that have brought us to this tipping point."[56]
>
> —Ruth Cox, president and executive director of the Fuel Cell & Hydrogen Energy Association.

Government Involvement Is Critical

Government involvement will be a key component in developing hydrogen power. In the future, government support for hydrogen power research is needed to improve production and storage technologies and make hydrogen power more efficient and economic. In addition, government support for up-front capital costs to build production facilities and distribution networks will help the hydrogen industry ramp up to commercial scale production in the coming years. Said Ruth Cox, "Our industry needs continued government support to cross the chasm and achieve broad-scale commercial deployment. . . . We can't afford to risk throwing away the considerable efforts that have brought us to this tipping point."[56]

Government Should Not Be Involved in Developing Hydrogen Power

"The evidence suggests that with respect to alternative energy development, government failure has in fact been a more persistent and costly problem than market failure."

—Peter Z. Grossman, the Clarence Efroymson Professor of Economics at Butler University.

Quoted in *Cato Journal*, "U.S. Energy Policy and the Presumption of Market Failure," Spring/Summer 2009. www.cato.org.

In August 2010 Beacon Power became one of the first companies to receive a DOE loan guarantee meant to support innovative and clean energy projects. Beacon Power's promising technology used large flywheels to store power and smooth dangerous electrical surges, which would be critical as fluctuating wind and solar sources provided more electricity. Beacon's technology appeared innovative, yet even with government support, it failed to attract private investors. Within a year the company filed for bankruptcy, leaving a debt of $39.1 million to the DOE and another $3.45 million to the state of Massachusetts.

As the Beacon Power failure demonstrates, state and federal governments can do more harm than good when getting involved in the development of speculative energy technologies. For this very reason, government should not be involved in the development of the hydrogen power industry. Although scientists are researching many potential hydrogen production and fuel cell technologies, it is unknown at present, which—if any—of these technologies will succeed. Given these uncertainties, the responsibility of developing the hydrogen power industry should fall on private companies and research facilities. Private energy and business experts are more qualified than politicians or government agencies to determine which technologies make sense. Margo Thorning, chief economist at the American Council for Capital Formation, explained, "If a renewable technology makes economic sense, the private sector will adopt it and it will succeed without mandates and subsidies. Federal and state governments should not mandate renewable energy."[57]

Governments around the world have spent billions of dollars on the development of hydrogen and fuel cell technology, yet there are few commercial successes to show for their investments. In the United States the DOE has spent more than $1 billion in research and development grants for hydrogen. A great deal more money and work is needed before hydrogen power and fuel cells can approach anything close to becoming a realistic energy alternative.

> "If a renewable technology makes economic sense, the private sector will adopt it and it will succeed without mandates and subsidies. Federal and state governments should not mandate renewable energy."[57]
>
> —Margo Thorning, chief economist at the American Council for Capital Formation.

Allow Free Market Forces to Work

Free market forces are the most effective way to determine which, if any, hydrogen and fuel cell technologies should be brought to market. In the free market only technologies that are economically viable will succeed. Private investors will fund and support winning technologies, while nonviable hydrogen technology will be allowed to fail. Nicolas D. Loris, a policy analyst at the Heritage Foundation who studies energy, environment, and regulation issues, explained:

There are plenty of technologies already developed to promote competition, and the one that emerges to provide a consistently affordable alternative to gasoline won't need the help of the government, because the profits will be enough incentive to drive production and lower costs, which will be enough incentive for the consumer to switch from a car that runs on gasoline to something

Hydrogen Fuel Funding Yields Few Results

From 2000 to 2010, the US Department of Energy has spent more than $2 billion on fuel cell and hydrogen research and development—with little to show for its efforts. As of 2012, one of the department's key goals, making hydrogen cost-competitive with gasoline, has not been achieved and is not expected to be in the near future. And, while the cost of building a hydrogen fuel cell vehicle has fallen in recent years, at $100,000 per car it is still far from being commercially viable.

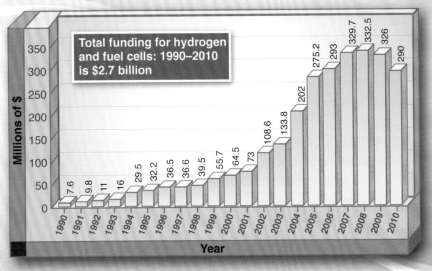

Total funding for hydrogen and fuel cells: 1990–2010 is $2.7 billion

Source: "Fuel Cell Technologies Program Record," Record #11004, United States Department of Energy, April 2011. www.hydrogen.energy.gov.

that is cheaper. . . . Good economic ideas can expand at rapid rates. Getting the government involved only impedes the process.[58]

In order to allow the free market to operate properly, the government should limit its funding of alternative energy sources, including hydrogen. Most government officials are not qualified to make scientific and business decisions on which technologies will succeed and should be funded. Bill Montgomery, managing director of the private-equity firm Quantum Energy Partners, believes that government should stay out of funding decisions and limit itself to establishing fair rules to encourage innovation. If the government intervenes as little as possible, it will allow the technologies to compete on merit alone in the free market, with more-qualified private investors deciding which companies and technologies to fund. "We have to accept the limitations of our own intelligence," said Montgomery. "Let the best technology flourish and win. The role of the government is not to pick winners and losers."[59]

Government Intervention Has Not Worked in the Past

History shows that government mandates and subsidies frequently do not work as intended. "Several recent bills would either subsidize or mandate alternative fuels and/or vehicles. However, the 30-plus-year history of federal attempts to encourage such alternatives includes numerous failures and few, if any, successes,"[60] wrote Loris and Ben Lieberman, senior policy analyst in energy and the environment at the Heritage Foundation.

One recent government energy market failure involved Solyndra, a solar technology company. In 2009 the federal government granted a $535 million federal loan guarantee to Solyndra. Some industry experts disagreed with the government's decision to finance Solyndra, because they questioned whether the company's technology was competitive against other companies with similar technologies. Shortly after receiving the federal money, the company ran into trouble when Chinese competitors flooded the market with a lower-cost product, decreasing the price Solyndra could charge for its solar panels. "To think [Solyndra] could compete on any basis, that took a very big leap of faith,"[61] said solar analyst Ramesh Misra. Stuck with high capital costs and low revenues, Solyndra declared bankruptcy in August 2011. "The Obama administration wasted $535 million in taxpayer funds in guaranteeing a loan to a firm that has proven to be unviable in the global market,"[62] said US representative Cliff Stearns.

The Solyndra failure demonstrates how the government can fail when picking alternative energy technologies to fund. With millions of dollars from the government, Solyndra was able to continue operating and spending taxpayer money on a technology that did not work in the marketplace. Without the government's money, it is likely that the company would have gone out of business earlier, saving the millions of dollars spent on a failing venture. "The lesson of Solyndra is that the government does not have the expertise to pick winners in the race to develop new energy sources,"[63] said William O'Keefe, CEO of the George C. Marshall Institute, a nonprofit scientific and public policy research organization.

Hydrogen Policy Failures

Within the hydrogen power industry, government intervention has also not worked as intended. One of the biggest government incentive programs for hydrogen power, the Hydrogen Fuel Initiative, earmarked $1.2 billion in research funds that would develop a hydrogen car. Between 2004 and 2008, the US government poured more than $1 billion into hydrogen, yet according to the Government Accountability Office, more than 25 percent of that money went to congressionally directed projects outside of the original research and development scope of the initiative. As of early 2012 one of the initiative's key goals of making hydrogen cost-competitive with gasoline still had not been achieved.

Despite receiving billions of dollars in federal subsidies, hydrogen power and hydrogen fuel cell vehicles remain too expensive for consumers. In addition, the infrastructure to support a hydrogen economy still does not exist. "It's just not a good use of taxpayer funds,"[64] said Joseph Romm, a senior fellow at the Center for American Progress and a former DOE official who supervised the hydrogen program during the Bill Clinton administration.

In recognition of the failure of government subsidies to help the hydrogen industry develop into a commercially viable energy carrier, secretary of energy Steven Chu slashed government funding into hydrogen research in 2009. Instead, Chu supports battery-run cars and biofuels as alternative fuels that are more likely to meet US energy and environmental goals in the near future. "If folks are frustrated with that position, I understand that. . . . We're trying to focus on the things that are going to make the impact in the time frame that matters, which is in the next five years,"[65] said Steven Chalk, Chu's deputy assistant secretary for renewable energy.

> **"The private sector is entirely capable of performing research into coal, nuclear, solar, and alternative energy sources for itself. Businesses will fund new technologies when there is a reasonable chance of commercial success, as they do in every other private industry."[67]**
>
> —Chris Edwards, an analyst for the Cato Institute, a public policy research institution.

Government subsidies for hydrogen fuel cell development have been unnecessary and a wasteful use of taxpayer money. The private market is already working to develop and determine whether hydrogen will be a viable technology in the future. Fuel cells are already used in industrial applications. Major car companies are devoting their own time and money to researching hydrogen and fuel cells. "The technology doesn't need subsidies. . . . Congress should remove obstacles to conventional energy sources and leave alternative technologies to the private sector,"[66] wrote Tom Finnigan of the Heritage Foundation.

Limited Government Role

The role of government in hydrogen power development should be limited to ensuring a level playing field for all potential technologies. Then governments should sit on the sidelines and allow free market forces of innovation and competition to determine which technologies will best be able to drive the world's energy future. Chris Edwards, an analyst for the Cato Institute, a public policy research institution, wrote:

> Federal energy research should be phased-out as an unneeded cost in an era of massive government budget deficits. The private sector is entirely capable of performing research into coal, nuclear, solar, and alternative energy sources for itself. Businesses will fund new technologies when there is a reasonable chance of commercial success, as they do in every other private industry. Federal subsidies may even be actively damaging to our energy future by steering markets in the wrong direction, away from the best long-term energy solutions.[67]

Government intervention in the form of tax credits, loan guarantees, and other subsidies only serve to prop up technologies and companies that are not viable and serve as a barrier to true market innovation. "We are an energy rich nation and a nation that leads the world in innovation," William O'Keefe explained. "Private capital, market forces, our abundance of energy and economic and energy realities can lead to the development of new energy sources in time. Trying to force them into the market won't work."[68]

Source Notes

Overview: Visions of the Future: Hydrogen Power

1. Quoted in Honda, "Jack Cusick," September 16, 2009. http://auto mobiles.honda.com.
2. Quoted in Honda, "Jack Cusick."
3. Quoted in Honda, "Jack Cusick."
4. Quoted in Peter Hoffmann, *Tomorrow's Energy: Hydrogen, Fuel Cells, and the Prospects for a Cleaner Planet*. Cambridge, MA: MIT Press, 2012, p. 14.

Chapter One: Is Hydrogen Power Affordable?

5. Quoted in Lindsay Chappell, "Toyota Slashing Costs Ahead of Fuel-Cell Entry," p. 4. *Plastics News*, August 8, 2011.
6. Quoted in Chappell, "Toyota Slashing Costs Ahead of Fuel-Cell Entry."
7. Quoted in ScienceDaily, "Breakthrough in Designing Cheaper, More Efficient Catalysts for Fuel Cells," February 23, 2012. www.science daily.com.
8. Quoted in Chuck Squatriglia, "Discovery Could Make Fuel Cells Much Cheaper," *Wired*, April 22, 2011. www.wired.com.
9. Quoted in Jerry Garrett, "Detroit Auto Show: Toyota Promises 'Affordable' Hydrogen Fuel-Cell Vehicle," *Wheels* (blog), *New York Times*, January 11, 2010. http://wheels.blogs.nytimes.com.
10. Quoted in Jad Mouawad, "Pumping Hydrogen," *New York Times*, September 23, 2008. www.nytimes.com.
11. Quoted in Mouawad, "Pumping Hydrogen."
12. Quoted in US Department of Energy, "Energy Department Awards More than $7 Million for Innovative Hydrogen Storage Technologies in Fuel Cell Electric Vehicles," December 12, 2011. http://apps1.eere.energy.gov.
13. Quoted in Mouawad, "Pumping Hydrogen."

14. Quoted in Mouawad, "Pumping Hydrogen."

15. Quoted in *Scientific American*, "Will Germany Become First Nation with a Hydrogen Economy?," August 25, 2011. www.scientific american.com.

16. Quoted in Erik Sofge, "Why the Hydrogen Feud Needs to End: Analysis," *Popular Mechanics*, December 18, 2009. www.popular mechanics.com.

17. US Department of Energy, "Hydrogen Storage: Hydrogen Storage Challenges," March 8, 2011. www1.eere.energy.gov.

18. Quoted in Mouawad, "Pumping Hydrogen."

Chapter Two: How Does Hydrogen Power Impact the Environment?

19. Quoted in Fuel Cell Today, "Coca-Cola Officially Unveils Its Fuel Cell Forklift Fleet," February 10, 2012. www.fuelcelltoday.com.

20. Quoted in Paul Hockenos, "Tomorrow's Energy: A Strong Case for Hydrogen," *National*, March 23, 2012. www.thenational.ae.

21. Quoted in National Renewable Energy Laboratory, "Low Emission Cars Under NREL's Microscope," August 17, 2011. www.nrel.gov.

22. Quoted in Steve Esack, "Air Products Wants to Supply California Drivers with Hydrogen," *Allentown (PA) Morning Call*, March 11, 2012. www.mcall.com.

23. Quoted in Wendy Koch, "Report: U.S. Coal Power Plants Emit Toxic Air Pollutants," *USA Today*, March 8, 2011. http://content .usatoday.com.

24. Quoted in Lauren Gravitz, "Cleaning Your Streets with the Power of Hydrogen," CoExist, 2012. www.fastcoexist.com.

25. Quoted in Reason Foundation, "Study: Hydrogen Cars Don't Reduce Greenhouse Gas Emissions," November 1, 2007. http://reason .org.

26. Quoted in SLAC National Accelerator Laboratory, "Hydrogen Fuel Tech Gets Boost from Low-Cost, Efficient Catalyst," May 2, 2011. http://home.slac.stanford.edu.

27. Quoted in Thomas K. Grose, "Hype or Hope?," *ASEE Prism*, September 2010, p. 47.

28. Quoted in Jim Motavalli, "Questions for Peter Hoffmann: A Hydrogen Advocate Whose Time May Have Come," *New York Times*, February 2, 2012. www.nytimes.com.

29. Patrick Coyle, "Fuel Cells to Power Cars," Suite 101.com, July 9, 2007. http://patrick-j-coyle.suite101.com.

30. Ron Pate, Mike Hightower, Chris Cameron, and Wayne Einfeld, "Overview of Energy-Water Interdependencies and the Emerging Energy Demands on Water Resources," Sandia National Laboratories, March 2007. www.circleofblue.org.

Chapter Three: Can Hydrogen Power Ever Replace Fossil Fuels?

31. Quoted in Abhilash Botekar, "Country's Energy Policy Has to Evolve with Time," *Times of India*, February 26, 2012. http://articles.time sofindia.indiatimes.com.

32. Daimler, "Fuels of the Future: New Fuels Will Replace Fossil Fuels," Sustainability Report, 2010. http://sustainability.daimler.com.

33. Quoted in Alan Ohnsman and Brian Wingfield, "Obama Hydrogen Fuel Failure Conceded by Chu Paring Budget: Cars," Bloomberg, June 14, 2011. www.bloomberg.com.

34. Quoted in AEG Power Solutions, "AEG Power Solutions Is Awarded a 6 Mw Contract for Hydrogen Electrolysis Process in Hybrid Power Generation Plant," press release, MarketWatch, April 23, 2012. www.marketwatch.com.

35. Quoted in James Kanter, "A Hydrogen Power Plant in Italy," *Green* (blog), *New York Times*, August 17, 2009. http://green.blogs.ny times.com.

36. Quoted in MSNBC.com, "Fuel Cells in the Home? Japan Is Big on the Idea," March 4, 2008. www.msnbc.msn.com.

37. Quoted in Fuel Cell & Hydrogen Energy Association, "Fuel Cell and Hydrogen Energy Association Looks Ahead; Welcomes Morry Markowitz as President & Executive Director," November 28, 2011. http://fchea.org.

38. Quoted in Douglas Newcomb, "Cleaner Air and Cleaner Streets Courtesy of Hydrogen," *Exhaust Notes* (blog), MSN Autos, March 14, 2012. http://editorial.autos.msn.com.

39. US Energy Information Administration, *The Impact of Increased Use of Hydrogen on Petroleum Consumption and Carbon Dioxide Emissions*, EV World, August 2008. www.evworld.com.

40. Chevron, "Energy Policy," May 2011. www.chevron.com.

41. Quoted in Grose, "Hype or Hope?," p. 47.

42. Quoted in Jim Motavalli, "With Cross-Country Trip, Hyundai Highlights Need for Hydrogen Fueling Infrastructure," *Wheels* (blog), *New York Times*, September 30, 2011. http://wheels.blogs.nytimes.com.

43. Quoted in Grose, "Hype or Hope?," p. 47.

44. Quoted in Ohnsman and Wingfield, "Obama Hydrogen Fuel Failure Conceded by Chu Paring Budget."

45. Quoted in Georgia Tech Research Institute, "Improving Fuel Cell Durability: Research into Better Fuel Cell Materials and Designs Starts with Studying Failures," November 28, 2007. www.gtri.gatech.edu.

Chapter Four: Should Government Play a Role in Developing Hydrogen Power?

46. Quoted in Fuel Cell & Hydrogen Energy Association, "Fuel Cell and Hydrogen Energy Association Launches Campaign to Transform the Energy Network," February 11, 2011. www.fchea.org.

47. Quoted in EurActiv, "Germany Blows Warm on Hydrogen Power," March 13, 2012. www.euractiv.com.

48. Quoted in EurActiv, "Germany Blows Warm on Hydrogen Power."

49. Electric Drive Transportation Association, National Hydrogen Association, and US Fuel Cell Council, "Hydrogen and Fuel Cell Industries Join Call to Increase Clean Energy Investment," press release, June 11, 2010. www.hpath.org.

50. Quoted in Eric Lipton and Clifford Krauss, "A Gold Rush of Subsidies in Clean Energy Search," *New York Times*, November 11, 2011. www.nytimes.com.

51. Fuel Cell & Hydrogen Energy Association, "Fuel Cell and Hydrogen Energy Association Launches Campaign to Transform the Energy Network."

52. Quoted in Lipton and Krauss, "A Gold Rush of Subsidies in Clean Energy Search."

53. Quoted in EurActiv, "Germany Blows Warm on Hydrogen Power."

54. Quoted in Ron Cogan, "Europe & Japan Push Fuel Cell Cars. Why Not the U.S.?," *Green Car*, October 19, 2009. www.greencar.com.

55. Hydrogen Link, "Danish Government to Launch Hydrogen Infrastructure Program and Continue FCEV Tax Exemptions Throughout 2015," press release, March 23, 2012. http://hydrogenlink.net.

56. Quoted in Fuel Cell & Hydrogen Energy Association, "Fuel Cell and Hydrogen Energy Association Launches Campaign to Transform the Energy Network."

57. Margo Thorning, "Stop DOE's Double Down on Risky Energy Ventures," *National Journal*, September 29, 2011. http://energy.national journal.com.

58. Nicolas D. Loris, "Government Shouldn't Decide What Cars Should Run On," *The Foundry* (blog), Heritage Foundation, June 7, 2011. http://blog.heritage.org.

59. Quoted in Gregory D.L. Morris, "What Is the Real Cost of Cheap Energy?," *Wharton Magazine*, Winter 2012, p. 68.

60. Ben Lieberman and Nicolas D. Loris, "Energy Policy: Let's Not Repeat the Mistakes of the '70s," Heritage Foundation, July 28, 2008. www.heritage.org.

61. Quoted in Debra Saunders, "Solyndra Debacle Spotlights Obama's Folly," *San Francisco Chronicle*, September 4, 2011. www.sfgate.com.

62. Quoted in Saunders, "Solyndra Debacle Spotlights Obama's Folly."

63. William O'Keefe, "Let Markets Shape Our Energy Future," *National Journal*, September 26, 2011. http://energy.nationaljournal.com.

64. Quoted in Ohnsman and Wingfield, "Obama Hydrogen Fuel Failure Conceded by Chu Paring Budget."

65. Quoted in Ohnsman and Wingfield, "Obama Hydrogen Fuel Failure Conceded by Chu Paring Budget."

66. Tom Finnigan, "Fuel Cell Subsidies," *The Foundry* (blog), Heritage Foundation, February 20, 2008. http://blog.heritage.org.

67. Chris Edwards, "Energy Subsidies," *Downsizing the Federal Government* (blog), Cato Institute, February 2009. www.downsizinggovern ment.org.

68. O'Keefe, "Let Markets Shape Our Energy Future."

Hydrogen Power Facts

Hydrogen Properties

- Hydrogen can be made from a wide variety of domestic, renewable resources such as solar, wind, biomass, and geothermal energy.
- Hydrogen is the universe's simplest atom: a single electron orbiting a single proton.
- Hydrogen has to be cooled to -423°F (-253°C) before it can be stored as a liquid.
- Once separated, hydrogen can take different forms; it can be a gas, liquid, or solid.

Hydrogen Production

- Enough hydrogen is produced in the United States every year to fuel 34 million fuel cell vehicles.
- Natural gas is an important resource for short-term hydrogen production.
- The DOE estimates that using natural gas to produce hydrogen in the near future would increase overall U.S. natural gas consumption by less than 3 percent.
- Patents for fuel cells grew 57 percent in 2010, outpacing other advanced energy technologies.
- A single fuel cell produces just over one volt of electricity, so hundreds are stacked together in vehicle and stationary fuel cell systems.
- Most US hydrogen is produced in three states: California, Louisiana, and Texas.
- Only 25 percent of the original electrical energy used to make hydrogen is turned back into electricity.

Hydrogen and the Environment

- Hydrogen is up to 25 percent more efficient than gasoline in conventional internal combustion engines and more than twice as efficient in fuel cell systems.

- A single fuel cell bus can save more than 30 tons (27.2 metric tons) of carbon dioxide annually compared with a diesel-powered bus.
- A 2010 McKinsey & Company study concluded that fuel cell electric vehicles are the best low-carbon vehicle in the medium- and large-car segments, which constitute about half the cars on the road and contribute 75 percent of all carbon dioxide emissions.
- Because fossil fuels generate more than 70 percent of electrical power in the United States, hydrogen produced from the electrical grid would still be a significant source of greenhouse gas.

Hydrogen Vehicles

- Honda spent $400 million to develop and build two hundred FCX Clarity fuel cell vehicles.
- Fuel cell vehicles are 50 percent more energy efficient than gasoline-powered cars.
- Fuel cell electric vehicles can achieve as much as 80 miles per gallon (34km/L) in gasoline equivalency, according to the Fuel Cell & Hydrogen Energy Association.

Hydrogen Infrastructure

- Twelve thousand hydrogen fueling stations would have the capacity to fuel 1 million hydrogen cars.
- A 44-ton (40-metric ton) vehicle that can carry enough gasoline to refuel eight hundred cars could only carry enough hydrogen to fuel eighty vehicles.
- Treating pipelines to protect them from high pressure and from becoming brittle would cost about $1 million per mile.

Related Organizations and Websites

American Hydrogen Association (AHA)
2350 W. Shangri La Rd.
Phoenix, AZ 85029
phone: (602) 328-4238
e-mail: 123goh2@gmail.com • website: www.clean-air.org

The mission of the AHA is to provide up-to-date information about worldwide developments concerning hydrogen, solar, wind, biomass, energy conversion, and the environment. It works with environmental groups, industry, communities, and schools to promote understanding of hydrogen technology.

California Fuel Cell Partnership (CFCP)
3300 Industrial Blvd., Suite 1000
West Sacramento, CA 95691
phone: (916) 371-2870
e-mail: info@cafcp.org • website: http://cafcp.org

The CFCP is committed to promoting fuel cell vehicles as a means of moving toward a sustainable energy future, increasing energy efficiency, and reducing or eliminating air pollution and greenhouse gas emissions. Its website features the latest news, research, and information about hydrogen fuel cell vehicles.

Cato Institute
1000 Massachusetts Ave. NW
Washington, DC 20001-5403
phone: (202) 842-0200 • fax (202) 842-3490
website: www.cato.org

The Cato Institute is a public policy research organization dedicated to the principles of individual liberty, limited government, free markets, and peace. Its scholars and analysts conduct independent, nonpartisan research on a wide range of policy issues, including hydrogen power and renewable energy. Its website provides publications on hydrogen power issues.

Fuel Cell & Hydrogen Energy Association (FCHEA)
1211 Connecticut Ave. NW, Suite 600
Washington, DC 20036
phone: (202) 261-1331
website: www.fchea.org

The FCHEA is the world's premier advocacy organization dedicated to the commercialization of fuel cells and hydrogen energy technologies. The group's website provides the latest news, fact sheets, and publications about fuel cell and hydrogen energy technologies.

International Association for Hydrogen Energy (IAHE)
5794 SW Fortieth St., #303
Miami, FL 33155
e-mail: info@iahe.org • website: www.iahe.org

The IAHE strives to advance the day when hydrogen energy will become the principal means by which the world will achieve its long-sought goal of abundant, clean energy. Toward this end, the association sponsors publications, international workshops, courses, and conferences.

National Renewable Energy Laboratory (NREL)
1617 Cole Blvd.
Golden, CO 80401
phone: (303) 275-3000
website: www.nrel.gov

The NREL is the DOE's laboratory for renewable energy research and development. Its website has maps, graphs, charts, and reports about renewable energy, including hydrogen power.

Natural Resources Defense Council (NRDC)
40 W. Twentieth St.
New York, NY 10011
phone: (212) 727-2700 • fax: (212) 727-1773
website: www.nrdc.org

The NRDC is a nonprofit environmental action group in the United States. NRDC's major efforts include curbing global warming and moving America beyond oil. Its website provides papers and fact sheets on a variety of energy topics, including hydrogen power.

Union of Concerned Scientists (UCS)
National Headquarters
Two Brattle Sq.
Cambridge, MA 02138-3780
phone: (617) 547-5552 • fax: (617) 864-9405
website: www.ucsusa.org

The UCS is the leading science-based nonprofit organization working for a healthy environment and a safer world. The website provides information and papers about hydrogen power and clean energy.

US Energy Information Administration (EIA)
1000 Independence Ave. SW
Washington, DC 20585
e-mail: infoctr@eia.gov • website: www.eia.gov

The EIA analyzes and distributes energy information to promote sound policies and the public understanding of energy and how it interacts with the economy and the environment. The EIA provides information covering energy production, demand, imports, exports, and prices. It prepares reports on topics of current interest, including hydrogen power and renewable energy.

US Environmental Protection Agency (EPA)
Ariel Rios Bldg.
1200 Pennsylvania Ave. NW
Washington, DC 20460
phone: (202) 272-0167
website: www.epa.gov

The EPA leads the nation in environmental science, research, and education efforts. The mission of the EPA is to protect human health and the environment. The EPA studies hydrogen power and its effect on the environment and recommends US policy. Its website provides detailed information about hydrogen power and its environmental pros and cons.

For Further Research

Books

Peggy Daniels Becker, *Alternative Energy*. Detroit: Greenhaven, 2010.

Matt Doeden, *Green Energy: Crucial Gains or Environmental Strains?* Minneapolis: Twenty-First Century, 2010.

Vikram Janardhan, *Energy Explained*. Lanham, MD: Rowman & Littlefield, 2011.

Stuart A. Kallen, *Hydrogen Power*. San Diego, CA: ReferencePoint, 2010.

Marilyn Nemzer, Deborah Page, and Anna Carter, *Energy for Keeps: Creating Clean Electricity from Renewable Resources*. Tiburon, CA: Energy Education Group, 2010.

John Tabak, *Natural Gas and Hydrogen*. New York: Facts On File, 2011.

Periodicals

Jonathan Adams, "Japan Leads the Race for a Hydrogen Fuel-Cell Car," *Christian Science Monitor*, February 1, 2010.

Keith Barry, "What the H? Everything You Need to Know About a Hydrogen-Fueled Future," *Car and Driver*, January 2012.

Jeff Tollefson, "Fuel of the Future?," *Nature*, April 29, 2010.

Internet Sources

California Fuel Cell Partnership, *How It Works*. www.cafcp.org/sites/files/How_it_works_booklet.pdf.

California Hydrogen Highway, State of California, "Frequently Asked Questions," March 15, 2010. www.hydrogenhighway.ca.gov/facts/faq/faq.htm.

Pew Center on Global Climate Change, *Hydrogen Fuel Cell Vehicles*, March 2011. www.pewclimate.org/docUploads/HydrogenFuelCellVehicles.pdf.

Websites

Alternative Fuels and Advanced Vehicles Data Center, US Department of Energy (www.afdc.energy.gov/afdc/fuels/hydrogen.html). The Alternative Fuels and Advanced Vehicles Data Center offers a collection of alternative fuel information, publications, data, and tools.

Fuel Cell Today (www.fuelcelltoday.com). Fuel Cell Today is a leading UK organization for market-based intelligence on the fuel cell industry. The group's website offers the latest news, industry events, and articles about fuel cells and hydrogen power.

Fuel Cell Technologies Program, US Department of Energy (www1 .eere.energy.gov/hydrogenandfuelcells/pubs_educational.html). This government website offers access to several easy-to-understand fact sheets and other information designed to introduce hydrogen and fuel cell technologies.

Index